OXFORD STUDENT TEXTS

Series Editor: Victor Lee

John Milton

Paradise Lost Books 1 and 2

Edited by Anna Baldwin

Oxford University Press

OXFORD
UNIVERSITY PRESS

Great Clarendon Street, Oxford OX2 6DP

Oxford University Press is a department of the University of Oxford.
It furthers the University's objective of excellence in research, scholarship,
and education by publishing worldwide in

Oxford   New York

Auckland   Cape Town   Dar es Salaam   Hong Kong   Karachi
Kuala Lumpur   Madrid   Melbourne   Mexico City   Nairobi
New Delhi   Shanghai   Taipei   Toronto

With offices in

Argentina   Austria   Brazil   Chile   Czech Republic   France   Greece
Guatemala   Hungary   Italy   Japan   Poland   Portugal   Singapore
South Korea   Switzerland   Thailand   Turkey   Ukraine   Vietnam

Oxford is a registered trade mark of Oxford University Press
in the UK and in certain other countries

British Library Cataloguing in Publication Data

Data available

ISBN: 978-0-19-832877-3

5 7 9 10 8 6 4

Typeset in India by TNQ

Printed in China by Printplus

Paper used in the production of this book is a natural, recyclable product made from wood
grown in sustainable forests. The manufacturing process conforms to the environmental
regulations of the country of origin.

The publishers would like to thank the following for permission to reproduce
photographs:

p2: Corbis/Hellier; p4: Corbis/Bettmann; p5: Corbis/Bettmann;
p8: Alamy/Paul Maguire; p161: British Library/Ms. Cotton Nero CIV fol 39r; p167:
Archivi Alinari; p171: The British Museum; p180: Huntington Library/SuperStock

Contents

Acknowledgements

Extracts from the *Authorized Version of the Bible (The King James Bible)*, the rights of which are vested in the Crown, are reproduced by permission of the Crown's Patentee, Cambridge University Press.

Extract from Aeschylus: *Prometheus Bound* in *Aeschylus: The Complete Greek Tragedies*, Volume 1, edited and translated by D. Grene and R. Lattimore (Chicago University Press, 1991), reprinted by permission of the publisher.

Extract from *Christopher Marlowe: Doctor Faustus and Other Plays* edited by David Bevington and Eric Rasmussen (Oxford World's Classics, 1995), reprinted by permission of Oxford University Press.

Extract from Vergil: *The Aeneid* translated by Robert Fitzgerald (Random House 1983, Vintage Classics, 1990), translation copyright © 1980, 1982, 1983 by Robert Fitzgerald, reprinted by permission of Random House, Inc.

We have tried to trace and contact all copyright holders before publication. If notified, we will be pleased to rectify any errors or omissions at the earliest opportunity.

Acknowledgements from Anna Baldwin

In memory of my father, John Barber, 1912–2005.

The task of re-editing *Paradise Lost Books 1 and 2* for this new series of Oxford Student Texts has been enormously assisted by the work of previous scholars. I would like to pay particular tribute to the editions of Books 1 and 2 by F.T. Prince (Oxford University Press, 1962), by John Broadbent (Cambridge University Press, 1972) and by Alastair Fowler, in *Milton: Paradise Lost* (Longman, 1968). I have quoted the prose works from *John Milton: Selected Prose* ed. C.A. Patrides (Penguin, 1974) and *The Milton Reading Room*, www.dartmouth.edu/~milton. Most of the secondary sources I have used are cited in Further Reading, page 193.

I would also like to thank Victor Lee and Jan Doorly for their meticulous but flexible editing.

Editors

Dr Victor Lee, the series editor, read English at University College, Cardiff. He was later awarded his doctorate at the University of Oxford. He has taught at secondary and tertiary level, working at the Open University for 27 years. Victor Lee's experience as an examiner is very wide. He has been, for example, a Chief Examiner in English A level for three different boards, stretching over a period of more than 30 years.

Anna Baldwin gained an MA and a PhD in English from Girton College, Cambridge, and went on to lecture in the Department of English and Related Literature at the University of York for 14 years. She has been teaching A level English Literature at a sixth-form college in Cambridge since 1994. Her other books include *Platonism and the English Imagination* (co-edited with Sarah Hutton, 1994), *A Guidebook to Piers Plowman* (Palgrave, 2007), and *Paradise Lost Book 9* (Oxford Student Texts, 2008).

Foreword

Oxford Student Texts are specifically aimed at presenting poetry and drama to an audience studying English literature at an advanced level. Each text is designed as an integrated whole consisting of four main parts. The first part sets the scene by discussing the context in which the work was written. The most important part of the book is the poetry or play itself, and it is suggested that the student read this first without consulting the Notes or other secondary sources. To encourage students to follow this advice, the Notes are placed together after the text, not alongside it. Where help is needed, the Notes and Interpretations sections provide it.

The Notes perform two functions. First, they provide information and explain allusions. Second (this is where they differ from most texts at this level), they often raise questions of central concern to the interpretation of the poetry or play being dealt with, particularly in the general note placed at the beginning of each set of notes.

The fourth part, the Interpretations section, deals with major issues of response to the particular selection of poetry or drama. One of the major aims of this part of the text is to emphasize that there is no one right answer to interpretation, but a series of approaches. Readers are given guidance as to what counts as evidence, but in the end left to make up their own minds as to which are the most suitable interpretations, or to add their own.

In these revised editions, the Interpretations section now addresses a wider range of issues. There is a more detailed treatment of context and critical history, for example. The section contains a number of activity-discussion sequences, although it must be stressed that these are optional. Significant issues about the poetry or play are raised, and readers are invited to tackle activities before proceeding to the discussion section, where possible responses to the questions raised are considered. Their main function is to engage readers actively in the ideas of the text.

At the end of each text there is also a list of Essay Questions. Whereas the activity-discussion sequences are aimed at increasing understanding of the literary work itself, these tasks are intended to help explore ideas about the poetry or play after the student has completed the reading of the work and the studying of the Notes and Interpretations. These tasks are particularly helpful for coursework projects or in preparing for an examination.

Victor Lee   *Series Editor*

John Milton in Context

Milton's life and involvement with politics

The poet John Milton (1608–74) was the son of another John Milton, a scrivener (a combination of lawyer and money-lender), who was not only financially very successful, but also a talented musician and composer. He sent his son to St Paul's School, where he learned to write in both Latin and Greek, and to Christ's College Cambridge (1625–32), where he came fourth in the University for his BA and then stayed on to take his MA. His father expected him to become a clergyman, as he was a fervent Christian, but his ideas were too independent and anti-royalist for the Church under Charles I (see page 7). So in 1632 he simply came home to Horton in Buckinghamshire to prepare himself to become a poet, learning French, Italian and Hebrew as well as reading even more deeply in classical literature in Latin and Greek.

Milton stayed there until he was nearly 30, and then travelled to Italy, where he was already famous for his Latin and Italian poetry. However, he became so concerned about the increasing political and religious turmoil in England that he returned the following year, and in 1641 decided to put poetry aside and become a kind of freelance commentator on events, in the hope that his stream of pamphlets would help to change government policy. His first volume of poems was, however, published in 1646, the year before the death of his father, who had supported him so faithfully.

One of the central issues in *Paradise Lost* is the nature of freedom, and it was freedom that Milton defended all his public life. His first pamphlets were aimed at the Church, first to free it from the tyranny of bishops and then, more personally, to advocate more liberal rules on divorce. He had separated from his first wife only weeks after marrying her, and during this period (1643–5) he published a series of Divorce Tracts which argued that one should be able to free oneself from an unworthy or incompatible partner. These prompted a storm of abuse (Parliament naming the first tract a 'wicked book'), and in another tract of the same period, the *Areopagitica* (1644), Milton defends the freedom of the press. Here he argues that the reader should not be over-protected, but be exposed to both good and evil in what he reads. He makes a vivid comparison between books and the fruit of the Tree of Knowledge forbidden to Man in the Garden of Eden:

> It was from out the rind of one apple tasted, that the knowledge of good and evil, as two twins cleaving together leapt forth into the World. And perhaps this is that doom that Adam fell into, of knowing good... by evil.

(Paraphrase: When Adam and Eve ate the apple, they gained knowledge of good and evil which, like conjoined twins, were born together; perhaps Adam's real punishment was that thereafter he should know good only by recognizing it is not evil.)

John Milton, depicted in an engraving of 1800

In *Paradise Lost*, published more than 20 years later, Milton is still defending the right of every reasonable creature to have freedom of choice, even if, like Satan or Adam, they choose to do evil.

The most important of Milton's public writings are political, and they reflect his increasing involvement in the opposition to King Charles I which developed during his 'eleven years' tyranny' of 1629–40. The Civil War which followed eventually resulted in the beheading of the king in 1649 and the period of 11 years when England was a republic (1649–60). Milton's important tract *Of the Tenure of Kings and Magistrates*, written during Charles I's trial, was one of the few contemporary publications to wholeheartedly support the execution of the king. But for Milton, abolishing kingship was a step back towards the original freedom of Adam:

> all men naturally were born free, being the image and resemblance of God himself, and were by privilege above all the creatures, born to command and not to obey: and... they lived so. Till from the root of Adam's transgression, [they fell] among themselves to do wrong and violence.

When, ten years later, Milton was to write *Paradise Lost*, he gave to Satan the same defence that he attacked God (the equivalent of Charles I) in order to give his followers freedom. We may dispute Satan's claim that God was a tyrant, and that in Hell *at least/We shall be free* (1:258–9), but the close correspondence between his political position and Milton's is an important source of its conviction and power.

Having executed the king in January 1649, the Council of State headed by Oliver Cromwell established a republican 'Commonwealth', and in March made Milton the Secretary for Foreign Tongues, with responsibility for translating documents into Latin – the *lingua franca* of Europe – and for explaining and justifying their actions both at home and abroad.

A print depicting the execution of Charles I in Whitehall
on 30 January 1649

Until 1655 Milton worked tirelessly to support the Commonwealth, publishing (among many other tracts) two *Defences of the English People* (in 1651 and 1654), which explained what the Commonwealth was trying to achieve. But privately he, like many of the English people, was becoming increasingly dissatisfied with it. Instead of giving men greater political responsibility, Cromwell's authority as a military dictator curtailed their freedom. He refused to recognize the decisions of Parliament when he did not agree with them, delayed holding another election until 1656, and then banned about 100 new members from attending the new Parliament. Cromwell's interference with individual lifestyles is discussed in the next section. There seemed no way of restraining him and his Council of State from arbitrary rule, and from 1658 Milton, who was now blind, increasingly spent time on *Paradise Lost* rather than defending a regime in which he could no longer believe, and a ruler who had become as much a tyrant as the king he had deposed. Instead, Milton put Cromwell into his poem; Satan has much in common with this gifted but flawed leader, and indeed with Milton himself, the eloquent rebel.

Oliver Cromwell, in an engraving depicting him in his armour

Cromwell's personal power had weakened the Commonwealth itself; when he died in 1658 it fell apart, and the movement to recall the executed king's son from exile in France became irresistible. The monarchy was restored when Charles II became king in 1660. Milton, again like Satan himself, refused to *bow and sue for grace* (1:111), but instead published a defence of republicanism in *A Ready and Easy Way to Establish a Free Commonwealth*, which asserts that no-one can be free under a monarchy. In consequence he was specifically excluded from the Charles II's official pardon for participants in the rebellion or the subsequent governments, and was thrown into prison. His life was spared, following the intervention of friends who included fellow poet Andrew Marvell; his opponents in any case believed that God himself had punished Milton with blindness for supporting the execution of the monarch. He was allowed to retire quietly, and married for a third time in 1663.

He occupied himself in writing poetry, history and theology, often returning in it to the thoughts and experiences which had preoccupied him during the most politically active period of his life. It took him seven years to complete his masterpiece, *Paradise Lost*, which was published in ten books in the first edition of

1667 (the basis for this text). A second edition in 12 books appeared in 1674, the year of his death; his payment for both was only £15. Milton's other mature works include *Samson Agonistes*, in which the blind hero complains of the degenerate nation which allows a tyranny to return:

> But what more oft in Nations grown corrupt,
> And by their vices brought to servitude,
> Than to love Bondage more than Liberty,
> Bondage with ease than strenuous Liberty

> (268–71)

When you are reading the speeches of Satan's followers in Hell, ask yourself whether they too seem to be embracing *Bondage with ease*, or whether they are more free in Hell, away from God, as Satan constantly claims.

Another of Milton's late works is *Paradise Regained*, a 'brief epic' in four books which shows Christ refuting Satan in the wilderness and so restoring man to Heaven. These works record how triumph can be seized out of personal agony – a triumph that Milton's life itself reflects.

Milton and the Puritans

The desire for religious freedom was as much a part of the English revolutionaries' original aims as the desire for political freedom. When Henry VIII passed his Act of Supremacy in 1534 he achieved freedom for the new protestant Church of England (the Anglicans) from the Catholic Church headed by the Pope. One difference that this change made to ordinary people's lives was that they were allowed to read the Bible for themselves in their own language. Later, in 1611, James I ordered that a copy of his English Bible should be placed in every Church (this *Authorized Version* is the translation Milton uses and is the version used in the Appendix).

This new independence from the intellectual control of priests encouraged many groups to work out their own kind of Christianity. The oddities of Milton's personal religion (described below) were therefore characteristic of an age where there existed numerous independent sects, such as the Baptists, Quakers, and Presbyterians, some of which followed the principles laid down by John Calvin in his 'Reformed' Church of sixteenth-century Geneva rather than the more 'Lutheran' beliefs of Anglicanism.

English Calvinists are often grouped under the generic term 'Puritans' because they expected their members to aspire to a high standard of virtue or purity as evidence that they had already been 'elected' by God to Heaven. (This was a doctrine to which the liberty-loving Milton did not subscribe – indeed he makes Satan claim to be predetermined for Hell.) Much of the wealth of the Church had been stripped away by Henry VIII when he dissolved the monasteries, and Puritans took this further by making plainness and simple living part of their creed. The Puritans of Cromwell's Model Army broke the stained glass in the churches and destroyed any paintings of saints remaining from the Reformation, which is why so few of England's churches retain their priceless inheritance of medieval stained glass.

Milton, though too independent to be a member of any particular sect, shares this new taste for religious simplicity. When you come to the passages describing the building of the infernal council chamber, Pandæmonium (1:713–30), and Satan's enthronement within it (2:1–10), look out for words suggesting wealth and display. Although the building itself is clearly a pagan temple, might Milton also have in mind the classical architecture and lavish decoration he had seen at St Peter's in Rome, where the Pope was enthroned (see page 8)? The English dislike of Catholicism was of course political as well as aesthetic (the Stuart kings were regarded as too sympathetic to the Catholics in France and Spain), and even Milton's pleas for religious toleration stopped short of allowing Catholics to worship freely.

The Papal Altar in St Peter's Basilica, Rome

Although in theory tolerant of the new Churches, and allowing Jews to return to the country after their centuries of exile, Cromwell and his ministers began to reorganize the Anglican Church, and tried to impose a rigorously Puritan way of life on everybody. In 1655 local 'major generals' were employed to check that people were attending church regularly, and not going to parties or horse-races, or to the theatres, supposedly closed since 1642. They encouraged the high moral standards felt to be a hallmark of Puritans, together with plain living, hard work, and independence, as Calvin had done in Geneva. Compare this list of Puritan values with those given by Mammon in his speech in Pandæmonium (2:249–62). Of course it is ironic that a character whose very name means 'wealth' should suggest a Puritan way of life in Hell; why does he do so? Certainly it was Milton's experience that Cromwell's imposed Puritanism pushed the English away from republicanism, and towards the movement to restore the monarch.

One of Charles II's first acts on coming to the throne was to reopen the theatres; he loved pomp and display, and even filled the London fountains with wine on public occasions. Charles tried also to restrict the independent sects, imprisoning men like John Bunyan the Baptist, but he could not put the clock back any more than Mary I had done when she tried to restore Catholicism in 1555; from 1672, religious toleration became part of royal policy. Milton, author of *A Treatise of Civil Power... showing that it is not lawful for any power on earth to compel in matters of religion* (1659) must have quietly rejoiced.

The context of Books 1 and 2 in the whole poem

Milton starts his poem, as Homer did his epics, in the middle of events (*in media res*), with Satan, the prince of Hell, lying with his followers on the burning lake in the centre of Hell, where they have been hurled by God for attempting to overthrow him. Satan vows revenge and rallies his followers, and together they build the council chamber of Pandæmonium, where they debate what to do next. The other devils want to abandon the fight against God, but Satan (through his second in command, Beëlzebub) persuades them to send him on a mission to corrupt God's new creation, his *darling sons* or Mankind, as this will be easier than open warfare and more likely to damage God's interests.

Satan flies off to Earth, meeting his daughter Sin and their son Death at the gates of Hell, and persuading them to help him on his way.

In Book 3 the scene changes to Heaven. God and his Son Jesus watch what the devils are doing and explain how good will be brought out of evil, the Son offering himself as a sacrifice, and God deciding to send the archangel Raphael to Earth to warn Adam and Eve of the danger.

Book 4 introduces us both to Satan's real character, in a wonderful soliloquy at the edge of the universe, and to Adam and Eve in Paradise. The Garden of Eden is described, and Adam and Eve praise God and make love innocently. Satan tries to tempt Eve through entering her dream, but is chased away by the archangel Gabriel.

In Books 5–8, Raphael visits Adam and Eve and tells them the story of Satan's jealousy of the newly begotten Son of God, and how he made his own division of angels (apart from one individual) resentful and rebellious, and led them in the war in Heaven which resulted in their expulsion. Raphael then describes the creation of the Earth, and promises Adam and Eve that their obedience will be rewarded with a gradual ascent to Heaven. He warns them about Satan's presence and his plans to seduce them from obedience, in order that God should be forced by his own justice to make them share Satan's punishment.

In Book 9 Milton describes how Eve persuades Adam to let her work in the garden alone, how she meets and is flattered by Satan disguised as the serpent, and is finally persuaded to eat the fruit of the forbidden tree. When she offers some to Adam, he decides to eat it in order to die with her. Both of them are intoxicated by the fruit and make love lasciviously, though their excitement is followed by a loathing of themselves and each other.

In Book 10 we see Sin and Death building a broad bridge to join Earth to Hell, and Satan returning to Hell where he and the other fallen angels are humiliated by being temporarily transformed into serpents. The Earth is made a much more difficult and uncomfortable place both by angels sent by God, and by the new presence of Sin and Death. God sends his Son to judge but also to comfort the sinful pair and, once alone, Adam both condemns himself and blames Eve for their predicament. His despair is alleviated by Eve, who asks Adam for pardon, and so shows him the way to effect a reconciliation with God; in this crucial way their Fall differs from Satan's.

In Books 11 and 12 God accepts Adam and Eve's repentance, and the archangel Michael is sent to show them both the hideous effects of the Fall in terms of human suffering and disease, and their eventual redemption by the Son of God, who will be born on Earth as the descendant of Eve. Finally he sends them out into the fallen world:

> Some natural tears they dropped, but wiped them soon;
> The world was all before them, where to choose
> Their place of rest, and Providence their guide;
> They hand in hand with wandering steps and slow,
> Through Eden took their solitary way.

(12:645–9)

Milton's ideas on Heaven, Hell, angels and chaos

The action of Books 1 and 2 does not take place within the universe but outside it. From reading Book 2 it is clear that the universe is only a small part of an infinite and eternal space, of which the upper part is Heaven, which has limits, and the lower part Chaos, which has no limit. At a great distance below Heaven is placed Hell, which is walled and gated, but also seems to have no limit.

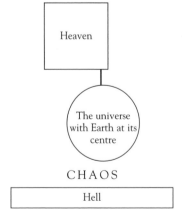

A sketch of Milton's universe

We should read this cosmology as a poetic myth, as it expresses neither the 'truth' of the Bible nor of contemporary science. Milton had visited Galileo (see Note to 1:287–91) and used his telescope to see into the real universe, and indeed his description of the vast but not empty Chaos in Book 2 has some of the characteristics of outer space as we understand it. But the universe in the poem is full of features which make poetic rather than scientific sense: the characters of Chaos and Night, the golden chain linking Earth to Heaven, and so on. In Book 10 the vast chasm of Chaos is even crossed by a bridge made by Sin and Death, which makes literal one of Jesus's sayings. Indeed the Hell described in Books 1 and 2 can itself be seen as a literal expression of the fallen angels' alienation and despair, its flames created when Satan's daughter Sin bursts from his own head (2:752–8) and its rivers and monsters reflecting the passions and self-contradictions of his mind (2:575–81, 624–8).

Milton's story of the Fall of the rebel angels in *Paradise Lost*, though derived from influential theologians like the fourth-century St Augustine of Hippo, is also unorthodox. Using passages from the biblical books of Isaiah and Revelation, Augustine had taught that the angels were divided into seven divisions or 'orders', each under a different archangel; the leading archangel was called Lucifer (bearer of light). Lucifer's pride (exacerbated in Milton's version, though not in most Christian theology, by finding himself placed below a newly begotten Christ) persuaded him and his own division of angels to rebel. After a great war in Heaven (see Revelation 12:7–9), the rebellious angels were thrust out and fell to the Hell that God had prepared for them, changing both their shape and their names; Lucifer became Satan.

Satan decided to revenge himself on God by corrupting humankind, the foremost creatures of God's newly made universe. He entered the body of a serpent and tempted Eve, and through her Adam, to eat the fruit of the one tree they had been forbidden to touch. Eve was persuaded that this fruit would make her like a god, and so her Fall imitates Lucifer's in being caused by pride and disobedience. Adam and Eve together with all their descendants are punished by death and residence after death in Hell, but Jesus's innocent sacrifice of himself has now 'atoned' for their Original Sin, and Christians who share the atonement through their baptism will be judged by God after death and can avoid Hell altogether.

Milton's ideas on the nature of good and evil

Milton's own ideas on the central issue of the nature of good and evil, of freedom, and of humankind's relation to God in general, were much influenced by St Augustine, the theologian who documented the Fall of Lucifer to become Satan, and identified him with the serpent of Genesis. St Augustine, himself influenced by neo-platonic ideas, had insisted that though goodness was a living reality, embodied in God, evil was not a power in itself, but a kind of negative impulse, an act of the will in preferring itself to God. To be happy as well as good, all creatures should accept their place in the hierarchy known as the 'Chain of Being', which looks something like this:

Heaven:	God
	Angels
Earth:	Man
	Woman
	Animals
	Plants
	Elements
Chaos:	Ingredients of nature without form
Hell:	Devils

All creatures should strive upwards towards God, and develop their potential by loving him (or loving goodness) as he loves them; hence this Chain of Being is sometimes called the Chain of Love. Evil creatures, however, choose to move downwards, away from God and true being. When Satan tried to depose God, he appeared to be trying to ascend upwards, but in reality he was replacing love of God by love of himself, and so instead of moving upwards began to circle around his own desires and to spiral downwards away from God. (The same thing will happen to Adam and Eve when they try to become gods by eating the forbidden fruit, but in fact lose their immortality because they replace the love of and obedience to God by the love of themselves.)

This self-reflective quality in evil is captured by Milton in the allegory of Sin: her marriages and births are all self-reflective, incestuous, unproductive and degenerative (see Interpretations page 179). Satan himself degenerates under our very eyes. Originally an archangel, made from the *empyreal substance* (1:117), that is to say, from the pure fire out of which Heaven itself is made, with a body which can change shape at will, and filled with heroic virtues, he seems in Book 1 to be scarcely *Less than archangel ruined* (1:593). But he begins to be corrupted by his own deceit; far from remaining *unchanged*, he is a flattering opportunist by the end of Book 2, and by Book 10 we are not sorry to see this cunning and spiteful being condemned to assume a snake's body against his will. Indeed two of the devil leaders, Belial and Mammon, actually encourage this process in themselves, avoiding pain in Hell by becoming more like Hell, and so degenerating from their original being. Like the English people Milton castigates in *Samson Agonistes* (see page 6 above), they love *Bondage with ease* more than *strenuous Liberty*, and have lost the freedom to move up through the Chain of Being. If Adam and Eve had remained obedient to God, they would have risen to rejoin the angels in Heaven, as Raphael promises:

> And from these corporal nutriments perhaps
> Your bodies may at last turn all to spirit,
> Improved by tract of time, and winged ascend
> Ethereal, as we
>
> (5:496–9)

It is for this reason that in *Paradise Lost* Milton shows the Fall of Man not as a necessary stage in our development, as he had in the *Areopagitica* (see page 2 above), but as a tragedy.

Reasons for reading Milton today

When you first approach Milton, you may feel that the text is too difficult, too religious, and too far from your own concerns. To insist that it is the most wonderful literary text after Shakespeare is unlikely to convince you; tastes differ. To assert that Christianity is a central part of our culture and worth understanding is also something you might dispute. But after you have worked through the poem, I hope you will no longer say that it is irrelevant or detached from your own most personal concerns. It is a poem that tackles the central problems of our lives: why evil exists, how essentially it differs from goodness, and whether we are free to choose between them. These problems are raised in terms of a fantasy which is at once realistic and universal. The story of Satan, which occupies these two books, is about authority and revolt, heroism and deceit, and it is conveyed in a narrative style full of passionate energy.

A Note on the Text

The text is based on the first edition (1667). We have removed all capitals expect those denoting proper names (e.g. *Heaven* when it means God's home rather than the sky) and God himself (e.g. *the Thunderer*), all italics, and all archaic spellings and contractions of words except those which affect the metre (e.g. *th'Eternal*). We have followed John Broadbent (Cambridge University Press, 1972), though much more sparingly, in adding the occasional accent where a modern pronunciation would affect metre. Punctuation has been retained (except for the addition of one or two question marks and full stops), but as Milton used commas, semi-colons, colons and full-stops in ascending order to denote the length of the pauses the voice should make when reading the poem aloud, do not expect them to help very much with expressing the grammar.

To clarify the sense, the names of speakers have been added into the margin of the text. The Notes are divided into sections, and breaks in the text indicate where each section begins and ends.

Paradise Lost Books 1 and 2

The Argument to Book 1

This first book proposes, first in brief, the whole subject, Man's disobedience, and the loss thereupon of Paradise wherein he was placed: Then touches the prime cause of his fall, the serpent, or rather Satan in the serpent; who revolting from God, and drawing to his side many legions of angels, was by the command of God driven out of Heaven with all his crew into the great deep. Which action passed over, the poem hastes into the midst of things, presenting Satan with his angels now fallen into Hell, described here, not in the centre (for heaven and earth may be supposed as yet not made, certainly not yet accursed) but in a place of utter darkness, fitliest called Chaos: Here Satan with his angels lying on the burning lake, thunder-struck and astonished, after a certain space recovers, as from confusion, calls up him who next in order and dignity lay by him; they confer of their miserable fall. Satan awakens all his legions, who lay till then in the same manner confounded; they rise, their numbers, array of battle, their chief leaders named, according to the idols known afterwards in Canaan and the countries adjoining. To these Satan directs his speech, comforts them with hope yet of regaining Heaven, but tells them lastly of a new world and new kind of creature to be created, according to an ancient prophecy or report in Heaven; for that angels were long before this visible Creation, was the opinion of many ancient Fathers. To find out the truth of this prophecy, and what to determine thereon he refers to a full council. What his associates thence attempt. Pandemonium the palace of Satan rises, suddenly built out of the deep: The infernal peers there sit in council.

Of Man's first disobedience, and the fruit
Of that forbidden tree, whose mortal taste
Brought death into the world, and all our woe,
With loss of Eden, till one greater Man
5   Restore us, and regain the blissful seat,
Sing heavenly Muse, that on the secret top
Of Oreb, or of Sinai, didst inspire
That shepherd who first taught the chosen seed,
In the beginning how the heavens and earth
10   Rose out of Chaos; or if Sion hill
Delight thee more, and Siloa's brook that flowed
Fast by the oracle of God: I thence
Invoke thy aid to my adventurous song,
That with no middle flight intends to soar
15   Above th'Aonian mount, while it pursues
Things unattempted yet in prose or rhyme.
And chiefly thou O Spirit, that dost prefer
Before all temples th'upright heart and pure,
Instruct me, for thou know'st; thou from the first
20   Wast present, and with mighty wings outspread
Dove-like sat'st brooding on the vast abyss
And mad'st it pregnant: what in me is dark
Illumine, what is low raise and support;
That to the highth of this great argument
25   I may assert eternal Providence,
And justify the ways of God to men.

Say first, for Heaven hides nothing from thy view
Nor the deep tract of Hell, say first what cause
Moved our grandparents in that happy state,
30   Favoured of heaven so highly, to fall off
From their Creator, and transgress his will
For one restraint, lords of the world besides?
Who first seduced them to that foul revolt?
Th'infernal serpent; he it was, whose guile

35   Stirred up with envy and revenge, deceived
      The mother of Mankind, what time his pride
      Had cast him out from Heaven, with all his host
      Of rebel angels, by whose aid aspiring
      To set himself in glory above his peers,
40   He trusted to have equalled the most High,
      If he opposed; and with ambitious aim
      Against the throne and monarchy of God
      Raised impious war in heaven and battle proud
      With vain attempt. Him the Almighty Power
45   Hurled headlong flaming from th'ethereal sky
      With hideous ruin and combustion down
      To bottomless perdition, there to dwell
      In adamantine chains and penal fire,
      Who durst defy the Omnipotent to arms.

50   Nine times the space that measures day and night
      To mortal men, he with his horrid crew
      Lay vanquished, rolling in the fiery gulf
      Confounded though immortal. But his doom
      Reserved him to more wrath; for now the thought
55   Both of lost happiness and lasting pain
      Torments him; round he throws his baleful eyes
      That witnessed huge affliction and dismay
      Mixed with obdurate pride and steadfast hate:
      At once as far as angels' ken he views
60   The dismal situation waste and wild,
      A dungeon horrible, on all sides round
      As one great furnace flamed, yet from those flames
      No light, but rather darkness visible
      Served only to discover sights of woe,
65   Regions of sorrow, doleful shades, where peace
      And rest can never dwell, hope never comes
      That comes to all; but torture without end
      Still urges, and a fiery deluge, fed

With ever-burning sulphur unconsumed:
70   Such place eternal Justice had prepared
For those rebellious, here their prison ordained
In utter darkness, and their portion set
As far removed from God and light of heaven
As from the centre thrice to th'utmost pole.
75   O how unlike the place from whence they fell!
There the companions of his fall, o'erwhelmed
With floods and whirlwinds of tempestuous fire,
He soon discerns, and weltering by his side
One next himself in power, and next in crime,
80   Long after known in Palestine, and named
Beëlzebub. To whom the arch-enemy,
And thence in heaven called Satan, with bold words
Breaking the horrid silence thus began.

Satan   'If thou beest he; but O how fallen! how changed
85   From him, who in the happy realms of light

to B.   Clothed with transcendent brightness didst outshine
Myriads though bright: if he whom mutual league,
place   United thoughts and counsels, equal hope,   *state*
And hazard in the glorious enterprise,
90   Joined with me once, now misery hath joined
In equal ruin: into what pit thou seest
anthere From what highth fallen, so much the stronger proved
He with his thunder: and till then who knew
The force of those dire arms? Yet not for those
95   Nor what the potent Victor in his rage   *more*
Can else inflict, do I repent or change,
Though changed in outward lustre, that fixed mind
And high disdain, from sense of injured merit,
That with the mightiest raised me to contend,
100   And to the fierce contention brought along
myself and Innumerable force of spirits armed
That durst dislike his reign, and me preferring,

His utmost power with adverse power opposed
In dubious battle on the plains of heaven,
105 And shook his throne. What though the field be lost?
All is not lost; th'unconquerable will,
And study of revenge, immortal hate,
And courage never to submit or yield:
And what is else not to be overcome?
110 That glory never shall his wrath or might
Extort from me. To bow and sue for grace
With suppliant knee, and deify his power
Who from the terror of this arm so late
Doubted his empire, that were low indeed,
115 That were an ignominy and shame beneath
This downfall; since by fate the strength of gods
And this empyreal substance cannot fail,
Since through experience of this great event
In arms not worse, in foresight much advanced,
120 We may with more successful hope resolve
To wage by force or guile eternal war   *already worked*
Irreconcilable to our grand Foe,   *on r...*
Who now triumphs, and in th'excess of joy
Sole reigning holds the tyranny of Heaven.'
125   So spake the apostate angel, though in pain,
Vaunting aloud, but racked with deep despair:

And him thus answered soon his bold compeer.
Beëlzebub: 'O prince, O chief of many thronèd powers
That led th'embattled seraphim to war
130 Under thy conduct, and in dreadful deeds
Fearless, endangered heaven's perpetual King;
And put to proof his high supremacy,
Whether upheld by strength, or chance, or fate;
Too well I see and rue the dire event,
135 That with sad overthrow and foul defeat
Hath lost us heaven, and all this mighty host

In horrible destruction laid thus low,
As far as gods and heavenly essences
Can perish: for the mind and spirit remains
140   Invincible, and vigour soon returns,
Though all our glory extinct, and happy state
Here swallowed up in endless misery.
But what if he our Conqueror, (whom I now
Of force believe Almighty, since no less
145   Than such could have o'erpowered such force as ours)
Have left us this our spirit and strength entire
Strongly to suffer and support our pains,
That we may so suffice his vengeful ire,
Or do him mightier service as his thralls
150   By right of war, whate'er his business be
Here in the heart of Hell to work in fire,
Or do his errands in the gloomy deep;
What can it then avail though yet we feel
Strength undiminished, or eternal being
155   To undergo eternal punishment?'

Whereto with speedy words the arch-fiend replied.
Satan: 'Fallen cherub, to be weak is miserable
Doing or suffering: but of this be sure,
To do aught good never will be our task,
160   But ever to do ill our sole delight,
As being the contrary to his high will
Whom we resist. If then his Providence
Out of our evil seek to bring forth good,
Our labour must be to pervert that end,
165   And out of good still to find means of evil;
Which oft-times may succeed, so as perhaps
Shall grieve him, if I fail not, and disturb
His inmost counsels from their destined aim.
But see the angry Victor hath recalled
170   His ministers of vengeance and pursuit

Back to the gates of heaven: the sulphurous hail
Shot after us in storm, o'erblown hath laid
The fiery surge, that from the precipice
Of heaven received us falling, and the thunder,
175 Winged with red lightning and impetuous rage,
Perhaps hath spent his shafts, and ceases now
To bellow through the vast and boundless deep.
Let us not slip th'occasion, whether scorn,
Or satiate fury yield it from our Foe.
180 Seest thou yon dreary plain, forlorn and wild,
The seat of desolation, void of light,
Save what the glimmering of these livid flames
Casts pale and dreadful? Thither let us tend
From off the tossing of these fiery waves,
185 There rest, if any rest can harbour there,
And reassembling our afflicted powers,
Consult how we may henceforth most offend
Our Enemy, our own loss how repair,
How overcome this dire calamity,
190 What reinforcement we may gain from hope,
If not what resolution from despair.'

Thus Satan talking to his nearest mate
With head up-lift above the wave, and eyes
That sparkling blazed, his other parts besides
195 Prone on the flood, extended long and large
Lay floating many a rood, in bulk as huge
As whom the fables name of monstrous size,
Titanian, or Earth-born, that warred on Jove,
Briareos or Typhon, whom the den
200 By ancient Tarsus held, or that sea-beast
Leviathan, which God of all his works
Created hugest that swim th'ocean stream:
Him haply slumbering on the Norway foam
The pilot of some small night-foundered skiff,

205   Deeming some island, oft, as seamen tell,
              With fixèd anchor in his scaly rind
              Moors by his side under the lea, while night
              Invests the sea, and wishèd morn delays:
              So stretched out huge in length the arch-fiend lay

210   Chained on the burning lake, nor ever thence
              Had risen or heaved his head, but that the will
              And high permission of all-ruling Heaven
              Left him at large to his own dark designs,
              That with reiterated crimes he might

215   Heap on himself damnation, while he sought
              Evil to others, and enraged might see
              How all his malice served but to bring forth
              Infinite goodness, grace and mercy shown
              On Man by him seduced, but on himself

220   Treble confusion, wrath and vengeance poured.
              Forthwith upright he rears from off the pool
              His mighty stature; on each hand the flames
              Driven backward slope their pointing spires, and rolled
              In billows leave i'th'midst a horrid vale.

225   Then with expanded wings he steers his flight
              Aloft, incumbent on the dusky air
              That felt unusual weight, till on dry land
              He lights, if it were land that ever burned
              With solid, as the lake with liquid fire;

230   And such appeared in hue, as when the force
              Of subterranean wind transports a hill
              Torn from Pelorus, or the shattered side
              Of thundering Etna, whose combustible
              And fuelled entrails thence conceiving fire,

235   Sublimed with mineral fury, aid the winds,
              And leave a singèd bottom all involved
              With stench and smoke: such resting found the sole
              Of unblessed feet. Him followed his next mate,
              Both glorying to have scaped the Stygian flood

240   As gods, and by their own recovered strength,
           Not by the sufferance of supernal Power.

Satan: 'Is this the region, this the soil, the clime,'
           Said then the lost archangel, 'this the seat
           That we must change for Heaven, this mournful gloom
245   For that celestial light? Be it so, since he
           Who now is sovereign can dispose and bid
           What shall be right: farthest from him is best
           Whom reason hath equalled, force hath made supreme
           Above his equals. Farewell happy fields
250   Where joy for ever dwells: hail horrors, hail
           Infernal world, and thou profoundest Hell
           Receive thy new possessor: one who brings
           A mind not to be changed by place or time.
           The mind is its own place, and in itself
255   Can make a Heaven of Hell, a Hell of Heaven.
           What matter where, if I be still the same,
           And what I should be, all but less than he
           Whom thunder hath made greater? Here at least
           We shall be free; th'Almighty hath not built
260   Here for his envy, will not drive us hence:
           Here we may reign secure, and in my choice
           To reign is worth ambition though in Hell:
           Better to reign in Hell, than serve in Heaven.
           But wherefore let we then our faithful friends
265   Th'associates and co-partners of our loss
           Lie thus astonished on th'oblivious pool,
           And call them not to share with us their part
           In this unhappy mansion, or once more
           With rallied arms to try what may be yet
270   Regained in Heaven, or what more lost in Hell?,
             So Satan spake, and him Beëlzebub
           Thus answered.
Beëlzebub: 'Leader of those armies bright,

Which but th'Omnipotent none could have foiled,
If once they hear that voice, their liveliest pledge
275   Of hope in fears and dangers, heard so oft
In worst extremes, and on the perilous edge
Of battle when it raged, in all assaults
Their surest signal, they will soon resume
New courage and revive, though now they lie
280   Grovelling and prostrate on yon lake of fire,
As we erewhile, astounded and amazed,
No wonder, fallen such a pernicious highth.'

He scarce had ceased when the superior fiend
Was moving toward the shore; his ponderous shield
285   Ethereal temper, massy, large and round,
Behind him cast; the broad circumference
Hung on his shoulders like the moon, whose orb
Through optic glass the Tuscan artist views
At evening from the top of Fésolè,
290   Or in Valdarno, to descry new lands,
Rivers or mountains in her spotty globe.
His spear, to equal which the tallest pine
Hewn on Norwegian hills, to be the mast
On some great ammiral, were but a wand
295   He walked with to support uneasy steps
Over the burning marl, not like those steps
On heaven's azure, and the torrid clime
Smote on him sore besides, vaulted with fire;
Nathless he so endured, till on the beach
300   Of that inflamèd sea, he stood and called
His legions, angel forms, who lay entranced
Thick as autumnal leaves that strow the brooks
In Vallombrosa, where th'Etrurian shades
High overarched embower; or scattered sedge
305   Afloat, when with fierce winds Orion armed
Hath vexed the Red Sea coast, whose waves o'erthrew

Busiris and his Memphian chivalry,
While with perfidious hatred they pursued
The sojourners of Goshen, who beheld
310 From the safe shore their floating carcasses
And broken chariot wheels, so thick bestrown
Abject and lost lay these, covering the flood,
Under amazement of their hideous change.
He called so loud, that all the hollow deep
315 Of Hell resounded.

Satan: 'Princes, potentates,
Warriors, the flower of Heaven, once yours, now lost,
If such astonishment as this can seize
Eternal spirits; or have ye chosen this place
After the toil of battle to repose
320 Your wearied virtue, for the ease you find
To slumber here, as in the vales of Heaven?
Or in this abject posture have ye sworn
T'adore the Conqueror? who now beholds
Cherub and seraph rolling in the flood
325 With scattered arms and ensigns, till anon
His swift pursuers from Heaven gates discern
Th'advantage, and descending tread us down
Thus drooping, or with linkèd thunderbolts
Transfix us to the bottom of this gulf.
330 Awake, arise, or be for ever fallen.'

They heard, and were abashed, and up they sprung
Upon the wing, as when men wont to watch
On duty, sleeping found by whom they dread,
Rouse and bestir themselves ere well awake.
335 Nor did they not perceive the evil plight
In which they were, or the fierce pains not feel;
Yet to their general's voice they soon obeyed
Innumerable. As when the potent rod
Of Amram's son in Egypt's evil day

340   Waved round the coast, up called a pitchy cloud
        Of locusts, warping on the eastern wind,
        That o'er the realm of impious Pharaoh hung
        Like night, and darkened all the land of Nile:
        So numberless were those bad angels seen
345   Hovering on wing under the cope of Hell
        'Twixt upper, nether, and surrounding fires;
        Till, as a signal given, th'uplifted spear
        Of their great sultan waving to direct
        Their course, in even balance down they light
350   On the firm brimstone, and fill all the plain;
        A multitude, like which the populous North
        Poured never from her frozen loins, to pass
        Rhene or the Danaw, when her barbarous sons
        Came like a deluge on the South, and spread
355   Beneath Gibraltar to the Libyan sands.
        Forthwith from every squadron and each band
        The heads and leaders thither haste where stood
        Their great commander; godlike shapes and forms
        Excelling human, princely dignities,
360   And powers that erst in heaven sat on thrones;
        Though of their names in heavenly records now
        Be no memorial, blotted out and rased
        By their rebellion, from the Books of Life.
        Nor had they yet among the sons of Eve
365   Got them new names, till wandering o'er the Earth,
        Through God's high sufferance for the trial of Man,
        By falsities and lies the greatest part
        Of Mankind they corrupted to forsake
        God their creator, and th'invisible
370   Glory of him, that made them, to transform
        Oft to the image of a brute, adorned
        With gay religions full of pomp and gold,
        And devils to adore for deities:
        Then were they known to men by various names,

375   And various idols through the heathen world.

Say, Muse, their names then known, who first, who last,
Roused from the slumber on that fiery couch,
At their great emperor's call, as next in worth
Came singly where he stood on the bare strand,
380   While the promiscuous crowd stood yet aloof?
The chief were those who from the pit of Hell
Roaming to seek their prey on Earth, durst fix
Their seats long after next the seat of God,
Their altars by his altar, gods adored
385   Among the nations round, and durst abide
Jehovah thundering out of Sion, throned
Between the cherubim; yea, often placed
Within his sanctuary itself their shrines,
Abominations; and with cursèd things
390   His holy rites, and solemn feasts profaned,
And with their darkness durst affront his light.
First Moloch, horrid king besmeared with blood
Of human sacrifice, and parents' tears,
Though for the noise of drums and timbrels loud
395   Their children's cries unheard, that passed through fire
To his grim idol. Him the Ammonite
Worshipped in Rabba and her watery plain,
In Argob and in Basan, to the stream
Of utmost Arnon. Nor content with such
400   Audacious neighbourhood, the wisest heart
Of Solomon he led by fraud to build
His temple right against the temple of God
On that opprobrious hill, and made his grove
The pleasant valley of Hinnom, Tophet thence
405   And black Gehenna called, the type of Hell.
Next Chemos, th'obscene dread of Moab's sons,
From Aroar to Nebo, and the wild
Of southmost Abarim; in Hesebon

And Horonaïm, Seon's realm, beyond
410   The flowery dale of Sibma clad with vines,
And Elealè to th'asphaltic pool.
Peor his other name, when he enticed
Israel in Sittim on their march from Nile,
To do him wanton rites, which cost them woe.
415   Yet thence his lustful orgies he enlarged
Even to that hill of scandal, by the grove
Of Moloch homicide, lust hard by hate;
Till good Josiah drove them thence to Hell.
With these came they, who from the bordering flood
420   Of old Euphrates to the brook that parts
Egypt from Syrian ground, had general names
Of Baälim and Ashtaroth, those male,
These feminine. For spirits when they please
Can either sex assume, or both; so soft
425   And uncompounded is their essence pure,
Not tied or manacled with joint or limb,
Nor founded on the brittle strength of bones,
Like cumbrous flesh; but in what shape they choose
Dilated or condensed, bright or obscure,
430   Can execute their airy purposes,
And works of love or enmity fulfil.
For those the race of Israel oft forsook
Their living strength, and unfrequènted left
His righteous altar, bowing lowly down
435   To bestial gods; for which their heads as low
Bowed down in battle, sunk before the spear
Of despicable foes. With these in troop
Came Astoreth, whom the Phoenicians called
Astartè, queen of heaven, with crescent horns;
440   To whose bright image nightly by the moon
Sidonian virgins paid their vows and songs,
In Sion also not unsung, where stood
Her temple on th'offensive mountain, built

By that uxorious king, whose heart though large,
445 Beguiled by fair idolatresses, fell
To idols foul. Thammuz came next behind,
Whose annual wound in Lebanon allured
The Syrian damsels to lament his fate
In amorous ditties all a summer's day,
450 While smooth Adonis from his native rock
Ran purple to the sea, supposed with blood
Of Thammuz yearly wounded: the love-tale
Infected Sion's daughters with like heat,
Whose wanton passions in the sacred porch
455 Ezekiel saw, when by the vision led
His eye surveyed the dark idolatries
Of alienated Judah. Next came one
Who mourned in earnest, when the captive Ark
Maimed his brute image, head and hands lopped off
460 In his own temple, on the grunsel edge,
Where he fell flat, and shamed his worshippers:
Dagon his name, sea monster, upward man
And downward fish: yet had his temple high
Reared in Azotus, dreaded through the coast
465 Of Palestine, in Gath and Ascalon,
And Accaron and Gaza's frontier bounds.
Him followed Rimmon, whose delightful seat
Was fair Damascus, on the fertile banks
Of Abbana and Pharphar, lucid streams.
470 He also against the house of God was bold:
A leper once he lost and gained a king,
Ahaz his sottish conqueror, whom he drew
God's altar to disparage and displace
For one of Syrian mode, whereon to burn
475 His odious offerings, and adore the gods
Whom he had vanquished. After these appeared
A crew who under names of old renown,
Osiris, Isis, Orus and their train

With monstrous shapes and sorceries abused
480   Fanatic Egypt and her priests, to seek
Their wandering gods disguised in brutish forms
Rather than human. Nor did Israel scape
Th'infection when their borrowed gold composed
The calf in Oreb: and the rebel king
485   Doubled that sin in Bethel and in Dan,
Likening his Maker to the grazèd ox,
Jehovah, who in one night when he passed
From Egypt marching, equalled with one stroke
Both her first born and all her bleating gods.
490   Belial came last, than whom a spirit more lewd
Fell not from heaven, or more gross to love
Vice for itself: to him no temple stood
Or altar smoked; yet who more oft than he
In temples and at altars, when the priest
495   Turns atheist, as did Eli's sons, who filled
With lust and violence the house of God?
In courts and palaces he also reigns
And in luxurious cities, where the noise
Of riot ascends above their loftiest towers,
500   And injury and outrage: and when night
Darkens the streets, then wander forth the sons
Of Belial, flown with insolence and wine.
Witness the streets of Sodom, and that night
In Gibeah, when the hospitable door
505   Exposed a matron to avoid worse rape.
       These were the prime in order and in might;
The rest were long to tell, though far renowned,
The Ionian gods, of Javan's issue held
Gods, yet confessed later than Heaven and Earth
510   Their boasted parents; Titan Heaven's first born
With his enormous brood, and birthright seized
By younger Saturn, he from mightier Jove
His own and Rhea's son like measure found;

So Jove usurping reigned: these first in Crete
515   And Ida known, thence on the snowy top
Of cold Olympus ruled the middle air
Their highest heaven; or on the Delphian cliff,
Or in Dodona, and through all the bounds
Of Doric land; or who with Saturn old
520   Fled over Adria to th'Hesperian fields,
And o'er the Celtic roamed the utmost isles.

Satan : recovering Pride

All these and more came flocking; but with looks
Downcast and damp, yet such wherein appeared
Obscure some glimpse of joy, to have found their chief
525   Not in despair, to have found themselves not lost
In loss itself; which on his countenance cast
Like doubtful hue: but he his wonted pride
Soon recollecting, with high words, that bore
Semblance of worth, not substance, gently raised
530   Their fainting courage, and dispelled their fears.
Then straight commands that, at the warlike sound
Of trumpets loud and clarions, be upreared
His mighty standard; that proud honour claimed
Azazel as his right, a cherub tall:
535   Who forthwith from the glittering staff unfurled
Th'imperial ensign, which full high advanced
Shone like a meteor streaming to the wind
With gems and golden lustre rich emblazed,
Seraphic arms and trophies: all the while   *sound*
540   Sonorous metal blowing martial sounds:
At which the universal host upsent
A shout that tore Hell's concave, and beyond
Frighted the reign of Chaos and old Night.
All in a moment through the gloom were seen
545   Ten thousand banners rise into the air
With orient colours waving: with them rose
A forest huge of spears: and thronging helms

Appeared, and serried shields in thick array
Of depth immeasurable: anon they move
550   In perfect phalanx to the Dorian mood
Of flutes and soft recorders; such as raised
To highth of noblest temper heroes old
Arming to battle, and in stead of rage
Deliberate valour breathed, firm and unmoved
555   With dread of death to flight or foul retreat;
Nor wanting power to mitigate and swage
With solemn touches, troubled thoughts, and chase
Anguish and doubt and fear and sorrow and pain
From mortal or immortal minds. Thus they
560   Breathing united force with fixèd thought
Moved on in silence to soft pipes that charmed
Their painful steps o'er the burnt soil; and now
Advanced in view they stand, a horrid front
Of dreadful length and dazzling arms, in guise
565   Of warriors old with ordered spear and shield,
Awaiting what command their mighty chief
Had to impose. He through the armed files
Darts his experienced eye, and soon traverse
The whole battalion views, their order due,
570   Their visages and stature as of gods,
Their number last he sums. And now his heart
Distends with pride, and hardening in his strength
Glories: for never since created Man,
Met such embodied force, as named with these
575   Could merit more than that small infantry
Warred on by cranes: though all the giant brood
Of Phlegra with th'heroic race were joined
That fought at Thebes and Ilium, on each side
Mixed with auxiliar gods; and what resounds
580   In fable or romance of Uther's son
Begirt with British and Armoric knights;
And all who since, baptized or infidel

Jousted in Aspramont or Montalban,
Damasco, or Marocco, or Trebisond,
585   Or whom Biserta sent from Afric shore
When Charlemain with all his peerage fell,
By Fontarabbia. ♪

                Thus far these beyond
Compare of mortal prowess, yet observed
Their dread commander: he above the rest
590   In shape and gesture proudly eminent
Stood like a tower; his form had yet not lost
All her original brightness, nor appeared
Less than archangel ruined, and th'excess
Of glory obscured: as when the sun new risen
595   Looks through the horizontal misty air
Shorn of his beams, or from behind the moon
In dim eclipse disastrous twilight sheds
On half the nations, and with fear of change
Perplexes monarchs. Darkened so, yet shone
600   Above them all th'archangel: but his face
Deep scars of thunder had entrenched, and care
Sat on his faded cheek, but under brows
Of dauntless courage, and considerate pride
Waiting revenge: cruel his eye, but cast
605   Signs of remorse and passion to behold
The fellows of his crime, the followers rather
(Far other once beheld in bliss) condemned
For ever now to have their lot in pain,
Millions of spirits for his fault amerced
610   Of Heaven, and from eternal splendours flung
For his revolt, yet faithful how they stood,
Their glory withered. As when heaven's fire
Hath scathed the forest oaks, or mountain pines,
With singèd top their stately growth though bare
615   Stands on the blasted heath. He now prepared

To speak; whereat their doubled ranks they bend
From wing to wing, and half enclose him round
With all his peers: attention held them mute.
Thrice he essayed, and thrice in spite of scorn,
620 Tears such as angels weep, burst forth: at last
Words interwove with sighs found out their way.

Satan: 'O myriads of immortal spirits, O powers
Matchless, but with th'Almighty, and that strife
Was not inglorious, though th'event was dire,
625 As this place testifies, and this dire change
Hateful to utter: but what power of mind
Foreseeing or presaging, from the depth
Of knowledge past or present, could have feared,
How such united force of gods, how such
630 As stood like these, could ever know repulse?
For who can yet believe, though after loss,
That all these puissant legions, whose exile
Hath emptied Heaven, shall fail to re-ascend
Self-raised, and repossess their native seat?
635 For me be witness all the host of Heaven,
If counsels different, or danger shunned
By me, have lost our hopes. But he who reigns
Monarch in Heaven, till then as one secure
Sat on his throne, upheld by old repute,
640 Consent or custom, and his regal state
Put forth at full, but still his strength concealed,
Which tempted our attempt, and wrought our fall.
Henceforth his might we know, and know our own
So as not either to provoke, or dread
645 New war, provoked; our better part remains
To work in close design, by fraud or guile
What force effected not: that he no less
At length from us may find, who overcomes
By force, hath overcome but half his foe.

650   Space may produce new worlds; whereof so rife
        There went a fame in Heaven that he ere long
        Intended to create, and therein plant
        A generation, whom his choice regard
        Should favour equal to the sons of Heaven:
655   Thither, if but to pry, shall be perhaps
        Our first eruption, thither or elsewhere:
        For this infernal pit shall never hold
        Celestial spirits in bondage, nor th'abyss
        Long under darkness cover. But these thoughts
660   Full counsel must mature. Peace is despaired,
        For who can think submission? War then, war
        Open or understood, must be resolved.'
           He spake: and to confirm his words, out-flew
        Millions of flaming swords, drawn from the thighs
665   Of mighty cherubim; the sudden blaze
        Far round illumined Hell; highly they raged
        Against the Highest, and fierce with graspèd arms
        Clashed on their sounding shields the din of war,
        Hurling defiance toward the vault of heaven.

670   There stood a hill not far whose grisly top
        Belched fire and rolling smoke; the rest entire
        Shone with a glossy scurf, undoubted sign
        That in his womb was hid metallic ore,
        The work of sulphur. Thither winged with speed
675   A numerous brigad hastened. As when bands
        Of pioneers with spade and pickaxe armed
        Forerun the royal camp, to trench a field,
        Or cast a rampart. Mammon led them on,
        Mammon, the least erected spirit that fell
680   From Heaven, for even in Heaven his looks and thoughts
        Were always downward bent, admiring more
        The riches of Heaven's pavement, trodden gold,
        Than aught divine or holy else enjoyed

In vision beätific: by him first
685   Men also, and by his suggestion taught,
Ransacked the centre, and with impious hands
Rifled the bowels of their mother earth
For treasures better hid. Soon had his crew
Opened into the hill a spacious wound
690   And digged out ribs of gold. Let none admire
That riches grow in Hell; that soil may best
Deserve the precious bane. And here let those
Who boast in mortal things, and wondering tell
Of Babel, and the works of Memphian kings,
695   Learn how their greatest monuments of fame,
And strength and art are easily outdone
By spirits reprobate, and in an hour
What in an age they with incessant toil
And hands innumerable scarce perform.
700   Nigh on the plain in many cells prepared,
That underneath had veins of liquid fire
Sluiced from the lake, a second multitude
With wondrous art founded the massy ore,
Severing each kind, and scummed the bullion dross:
705   A third as soon had formed within the ground
A various mould, and from the boiling cells
By strange conveyance filled each hollow nook,
As in an organ from one blast of wind
To many a row of pipes the sound-board breathes.
710   Anon out of the earth a fabric huge
Rose like an exhalation, with the sound
Of dulcet symphonies and voices sweet,
Built like a temple, where pilasters round
Were set, and Doric pillars overlaid
715   With golden architrave; nor did there want
Cornice or frieze, with bossy sculptures graven,
The roof was fretted gold. Not Babylon,
Nor great Alcairo such magnificence

Equalled in all their glories, to enshrine
720   Belus or Serapis their gods, or seat
Their kings, when Egypt with Assyria strove,
In wealth and luxury. Th'ascending pile
Stood fixed her stately highth, and straight the doors
Opening their brazen folds discover wide
725   Within, her ample spaces, o'er the smooth
And level pavement: from the archèd roof
Pendant by subtle magic many a row
Of starry lamps and blazing cressets fed
With naphtha and asphaltus yielded light
730   As from a sky. The hasty multitude
Admiring entered, and the work some praise
And some the architect: his hand was known
In Heaven by many a towered structure high,
Where sceptred angels held their residence,
735   And sat as princes, whom the supreme King
Exalted to such power, and gave to rule,
Each in his hierarchy, the orders bright.
Nor was his name unheard or unadored
In ancient Greece; and in Ausonian land
740   Men called him Mulciber; and how he fell
From Heaven, they fabled, thrown by angry Jove
Sheer o'er the crystal battlements: from morn
To noon he fell, from noon to dewy eve,
A summer's day; and with the setting sun
745   Dropped from the zenith like a falling star,
On Lemnos th'Ægean isle: thus they relate,
Erring; for he with this rebellious rout
Fell long before; nor aught availed him now
To have built in Heaven high towers; nor did he scape
750   By all his engines, but was headlong sent
With his industrious crew to build in Hell.

Meanwhile the wingèd heralds by command

Of sovereign power, with awful ceremony
And trumpets' sound throughout the host proclaim
755   A solemn council forthwith to be held
At Pandæmonium, the high capital
Of Satan and his peers: their summons called
From every band and squarèd regiment
By place or choice the worthiest; they anon
760   With hundreds and with thousands trooping came
Attended: all access was thronged, the gates
And porches wide, but chief the spacious hall
(Though like a covered field, where champions bold
Wont ride in armed, and at the soldan's chair
765   Defied the best of paynim chivalry
To mortal combat or career with lance)
Thick swarmed, both on the ground and in the air,
Brushed with the hiss of rustling wings. As bees
In spring time, when the sun with Taurus rides,
770   Pour forth their populous youth about the hive
In clusters; they among fresh dews and flowers
Fly to and fro, or on the smoothèd plank,
The suburb of their straw-built citadel,
New rubbed with balm, expatiate and confer
775   Their state affairs. So thick the airy crowd
Swarmed and were straitened; till the signal given,
Behold a wonder! they but now who seemed
In bigness to surpass Earth's giant sons
Now less than smallest dwarfs, in narrow room
780   Throng numberless, like that pygmean race
Beyond the Indian mount, or fairy elves,
Whose midnight revels, by a forest side
Or fountain some belated peasant sees,
Or dreams he sees, while overhead the moon
785   Sits arbitress, and nearer to the Earth
Wheels her pale course, they on their mirth and dance
Intent, with jocund music charm his ear;

At once with joy and fear his heart rebounds.
Thus incorporeal spirits to smallest forms
790   Reduced their shapes immense, and were at large,
Though without number still amidst the hall
Of that infernal court. But far within
And in their own dimensions like themselves
The great seraphic lords and cherubim
795   In close recess and secret conclave sat
A thousand demi-gods on golden seats,
Frequent and full. After short silence then
And summons read, the great consult began.

The Argument to Book 2

The consultation begun, Satan debates whether another battle be to be hazarded for the recovery of Heaven: some advise it, others dissuade: A third proposal is preferred, mentioned before by Satan, to search the truth of that prophecy or tradition in Heaven concerning another world, and another kind of creature equal or not much inferior to themselves, about this time to be created: Their doubt who shall be sent on this difficult search: Satan their chief undertakes alone the voyage, is honoured and applauded. The council thus ended, the rest betake them several ways and to several employments, as their inclinations lead them, to entertain the time till Satan return. He passes on his journey to Hell gates, finds them shut, and who sat there to guard them, by whom at length they are opened, and discover to him the great gulf between Hell and Heaven; with what difficulty he passes through, directed by Chaos, the power of that place, to the sight of this new world which he sought.

High on a throne of royal state, which far
Outshone the wealth of Ormus and of Ind,
Or where the gorgeous East with richest hand
Showers on her kings barbaric pearl and gold,
5   Satan exalted sat, by merit raised
To that bad eminence; and from despair
Thus high uplifted beyond hope, aspires
Beyond thus high, insatiate to pursue
Vain war with Heaven, and by success untaught
10   His proud imaginations thus displayed.
Satan: 'Powers and Dominions, deities of heaven,
For since no deep within her gulf can hold
Immortal vigour, though oppressed and fallen,
I give not Heaven for lost. From this descent
15   Celestial virtues rising, will appear
More glorious and more dread than from no fall,
And trust themselves to fear no second fate:
Me though just right, and the fixed laws of Heaven
Did first create your leader, next, free choice,
20   With what besides, in counsel or in fight,
Hath been achieved of merit, yet this loss
Thus far at least recovered, hath much more
Established in a safe unenvied throne
Yielded with full consent. The happier state
25   In Heaven, which follows dignity, might draw
Envy from each inferior; but who here
Will envy whom the highest place exposes
Foremost to stand against the Thunderer's aim
Your bulwark, and condemns to greatest share
30   Of endless pain? where there is then no good
For which to strive, no strife can grow up there
From faction; for none sure will claim in Hell
Precédence, none, whose portion is so small
Of present pain, that with ambitious mind
35   Will covet more. With this advantage then

To union, and firm faith, and firm accord,
More than can be in Heaven, we now return
To claim our just inheritance of old,
Surer to prosper than prosperity
40 Could have assured us; and by what best way,
Whether of open war or covert guile,
We now debate; who can advise, may speak.'

He ceased, and next him Moloch, sceptred king
Stood up, the strongest and the fiercest spirit
45 That fought in Heaven; now fiercer by despair:
His trust was with th'Eternal to be deemed
Equal in strength, and rather than be less
Cared not to be at all; with that care lost
Went all his fear: of God, or Hell, or worse
50 He recked not, and these words thereafter spake.
Moloch: 'My sentence is for open war: of wiles,
More unexpert, I boast not: them let those
Contrive who need, or when they need, not now.
For while they sit contriving, shall the rest,
55 Millions that stand in arms, and longing wait
The signal to ascend, sit lingering here
Heaven's fugitives, and for their dwelling place
Accept this dark opprobrious den of shame,
The prison of his tyranny who reigns
60 By our delay? no, let us rather choose
Armed with Hell flames and fury all at once
O'er Heaven's high towers to force resistless way,
Turning our tortures into horrid arms
Against the Torturer; when to meet the noise
65 Of his almighty engine he shall hear
Infernal thunder, and for lightning see
Black fire and horror shot with equal rage
Among his angels; and his throne itself
Mixed with Tartarean sulphur, and strange fire,

70   His own invented torments. But perhaps
        The way seems difficult and steep to scale
        With upright wing against a higher foe.
        Let such bethink them, if the sleepy drench
        Of that forgetful lake benumb not still,
75   That in our proper motion we ascend
        Up to our native seat: descent and fall
        To us is adverse. Who but felt of late
        When the fierce foe hung on our broken rear
        Insulting, and pursued us through the deep,
80   With what compulsion and laborious flight
        We sunk thus low? Th'ascent is easy then;
        Th'event is feared; should we again provoke
        Our Stronger, some worse way his wrath may find
        To our destruction: if there be in Hell
85   Fear to be worse destroyed: what can be worse
        Than to dwell here, driven out from bliss, condemned
        In this abhorrèd deep to utter woe;
        Where pain of unextinguishable fire
        Must exercise us without hope of end
90   The vassals of his anger, when the scourge
        Inexorably, and the torturing hour
        Call us to penance? More destroyed than thus
        We should be quite abolished and expire.
        What fear we then? what doubt we to incense
95   His utmost ire? which to the highth enraged,
        Will either quite consume us, and reduce
        To nothing this essential, happier far
        Than miserable to have eternal being:
        Or if our substance be indeed divine,
100   And cannot cease to be, we are at worst
        On this side nothing; and by proof we feel
        Our power sufficient to disturb his Heaven,
        And with perpetual inroads to alarm,
        Though inaccessible, his fatal throne:

105   Which if not victory is yet revenge.'

     He ended frowning, and his look denounced
    Desperate revenge, and battle dangerous
    To less than gods. On th'other side up rose
    Belial, in act more graceful and humane;
110   A fairer person lost not Heaven; he seemed
    For dignity composed and high exploit:
    But all was false and hollow; though his tongue
    Dropped manna, and could make the worse appear
    The better reason, to perplex and dash
115   Maturest counsels: for his thoughts were low;
    To vice industrious, but to nobler deeds
    Timorous and slothful: yet he pleased the ear,
    And with persuasive accent thus began.
Belial: 'I should be much for open war, O peers,
120   As not behind in hate; if what was urged
    Main reason to persuade immediate war,
    Did not dissuade me most, and seem to cast
    Ominous conjecture on the whole success:
    When he who most excels in fact of arms,
125   In what he counsels and in what excels
    Mistrustful, grounds his courage on despair
    And utter dissolution, as the scope
    Of all his aim, after some dire revenge.
    First, what revenge? The towers of Heaven are filled
130   With armèd watch, that render all access
    Impregnable; oft on the bordering deep
    Encamp their legions, or with óbscure wing
    Scout far and wide into the realm of Night,
    Scorning surprise. Or could we break our way
135   By force, and at our heels all Hell should rise
    With blackest insurrection, to confound
    Heaven's purest light, yet our great Enemy
    All incorruptible would on his throne

Sit unpolluted, and th'ethereal mould
140 Incapable of stain would soon expel
Her mischief, and purge off the baser fire
Victorious. Thus repulsed, our final hope
Is flat despair: we must exasperate
Th'almighty Victor to spend all his rage,
145 And that must end us, that must be our cure,
To be no more; sad cure; for who would lose,
Though full of pain, this intellectual being,
Those thoughts that wander through eternity,
To perish rather, swallowed up and lost
150 In the wide womb of uncreated night,
Devoid of sense and motion? and who knows,
Let this be good, whether our angry Foe
Can give it, or will ever? how he can
Is doubtful; that he never will is sure.
155 Will he, so wise, let loose at once his ire,
Belike through impotence, or unaware,
To give his enemies their wish, and end
Them in his anger, whom his anger saves
To punish endless? wherefore cease we then?
160 Say they who counsel war, we are decreed,
Reserved and destined to eternal woe;
Whatever doing, what can we suffer more,
What can we suffer worse? is this then worst,
Thus sitting, thus consulting, thus in arms?
165 What when we fled amain, pursued and strook
With Heaven's afflicting thunder, and besought
The deep to shelter us? this Hell then seemed
A refuge from those wounds: or when we lay
Chained on the burning lake? that sure was worse.
170 What if the breath that kindled those grim fires
Awaked should blow them into sevenfold rage
And plunge us in the flames? or from above
Should intermitted vengeance arm again

His red right hand to plague us? what if all
175   Her stores were opened, and this firmament
Of Hell should spout her cataracts of fire,
Impendent horrors, threatening hideous fall
One day upon our heads; while we perhaps
Designing or exhorting glorious war,
180   Caught in a fiery tempest shall be hurled
Each on his rock transfixed, the sport and prey
Of racking whirlwinds, or for ever sunk
Under yon boiling ocean, wrapped in chains;
There to converse with everlasting groans,
185   Unrespited, unpitied, unreprieved,
Ages of hopeless end; this would be worse.
War therefore, open or concealed, alike
My voice dissuades; for what can force or guile
With him, or who deceive his mind, whose eye
190   Views all things at one view? he from Heaven's highth
All these our motions vain, sees and derides;
Not more almighty to resist our might
Than wise to frústrate all our plots and wiles.
Shall we then live thus vile, the race of Heaven
195   Thus trampled, thus expelled to suffer here
Chains and these torments? Better these than worse
By my advice; since fate inevitable
Subdues us, and omnipotent decree,
The Victor's will. To suffer, as to do,
200   Our strength is equal, nor the law unjust
That so ordains: this was at first resolved,
If we were wise, against so great a Foe
Contending, and so doubtful what might fall.
I laugh, when those who at the spear are bold
205   And venturous, if that fail them, shrink and fear
What yet they know must follow, to endure
Exile, or ignominy, or bonds, or pain,
The sentence of their conqueror. This is now

Our doom; which if we can sustain and bear,
210   Our súpreme Foe in time may much remit
His anger, and perhaps thus far removed
Not mind us not offending, satisfied
With what is punished; whence these raging fires
Will slacken, if his breath stir not their flames.
215   Our purer essence then will overcome
Their noxious vapour, or inured not feel,
Or changed at length, and to the place conformed
In temper and in nature, will receive
Familiar the fierce heat, and void of pain;
220   This horror will grow mild, this darkness light,
Besides what hope the never-ending flight
Of future days may bring, what chance, what change
Worth waiting, since our present lot appears
For happy though but ill, for ill not worst,
225   If we procure not to ourselves more woe.'
          Thus Belial with words clothed in reason's garb
Counselled ignoble ease, and peaceful sloth,
Not peace: and after him thus Mammon spake.

Mammon: 'Either to disenthrone the King of Heaven
230   We war, if war be best, or to regain
Our own right lost: him to unthrone we then
May hope when everlasting fate shall yield
To fickle chance, and Chaos judge the strife:
The former vain to hope argues as vain
235   The latter: for what place can be for us
Within Heaven's bound, unless Heaven's Lord
          supreme
We overpower? Suppose he should relent
And publish grace to all, on promise made
Of new subjection; with what eyes could we
240   Stand in his presence humble, and receive
Strict laws imposed, to celebrate his throne

With warbled hymns, and to his Godhead sing
Forced hallelujahs? while he lordly sits
Our envied Sovereign, and his altar breathes
245 Ambrosial odours and ambrosial flowers,
Our servile offerings. This must be our task
In Heaven, this our delight; how wearisome
Eternity so spent in worship paid
To whom we hate. Let us not then pursue
250 By force impossible, by leave obtained
Unacceptable, though in Heaven, our state
Of splendid vassalage, but rather seek
Our own good from ourselves, and from our own
Live to ourselves, though in this vast recess,
255 Free, and to none accountable, preferring
Hard liberty before the easy yoke
Of servile pomp. Our greatness will appear
Then most conspicuous, when great things of small,
Useful of hurtful, prosperous of adverse
260 We can create, and in what place so e'er
Thrive under evil, and work ease out of pain
Through labour and endurance. This deep world
Of darkness do we dread? How oft amidst
Thick clouds and dark doth Heaven's all-ruling
    Sire
265 Choose to reside, his glory unobscured,
And with the majesty of darkness round
Covers his throne; from whence deep thunders roar
Mustering their rage, and Heaven resembles Hell?
As he our darkness, cannot we his light
270 Imitate when we please? This desert soil
Wants not her hidden lustre, gems and gold;
Nor want we skill or art, from whence to raise
Magnificence; and what can Heaven show more?
Our torments also may in length of time
275 Become our elements, these piercing fires

As soft as now severe, our temper changed
Into their temper; which must needs remove
The sensible of pain. All things invite
To peaceful counsels, and the settled state
280   Of order, how in safety best we may
Compose our present evils, with regard
Of what we are and where, dismissing quite
All thoughts of war: ye have what I advise.'

He scarce had finished, when such murmur filled
285   Th'assembly, as when hollow rocks retain
The sound of blust'ring winds, which all night long
Had roused the sea, now with hoarse cadence lull
Seafaring men o'erwatched, whose bark by chance
Or pinnace anchors in a craggy bay
290   After the tempest: such applause was heard
As Mammon ended, and his sentence pleased,
Advising peace: for such another field
They dreaded worse than Hell: so much the fear
Of thunder and the sword of Michaël
295   Wrought still within them; and no less desire
To found this nether empire, which might rise
By policy, and long process of time,
In emulation opposite to Heaven.
Which when Beëlzebub perceived, than whom,
300   Satan except, none higher sat, with grave
Aspect he rose, and in his rising seemed
A pillar of state; deep on his front engraven
Deliberation sat and public care;
And princely counsel in his face yet shone,
305   Majestic though in ruin: sage he stood
With Atlantean shoulders fit to bear
The weight of mightiest monarchies; his look
Drew audience and attention still as night
Or summer's noontide air, while thus he spake.

310 **Beëlzebub:** 'Thrones and imperial powers, offspring of
        Heaven,
        Ethereal virtues; or these titles now
        Must we renounce, and changing style be called
        Princes of Hell? for so the popular vote
        Inclines, here to continue, and build up here
315   A growing empire; doubtless; while we dream,
        And know not that the King of Heaven hath doomed
        This place our dungeon, not our safe retreat
        Beyond his potent arm, to live exempt
        From Heaven's high jurisdiction, in new league
320   Banded against his throne, but to remain
        In strictest bondage, though thus far removed,
        Under th'inevitable curb, reserved
        His captive multitude: for he, be sure,
        In highth or depth, still first and last will reign
325   Sole King, and of his kingdom lose no part
        By our revolt, but over Hell extend
        His empire, and with iron sceptre rule
        Us here, as with his golden those in Heaven.
        What sit we then projecting peace and war?
330   War hath determined us, and foiled with loss
        Irreparable; terms of peace yet none
        Vouchsafed or sought; for what peace will be given
        To us enslaved, but custody severe,
        And stripes, and arbitrary punishment
335   Inflicted? and what peace can we return,
        But to our power hostility and hate,
        Untamed reluctance, and revenge though slow,
        Yet ever plotting how the Conqueror least
        May reap his conquest, and may least rejoice
340   In doing what we most in suffering feel?
        Nor will occasion want, nor shall we need
        With dangerous expedition to invade
        Heaven, whose high walls fear no assault or siege,

Or ambush from the deep. What if we find
345 Some easier enterprise? There is a place
(If ancient and prophetic fame in Heaven
Err not) another world, the happy seat
Of some new race called Man, about this time
To be created like to us, though less
350 In power and excellence, but favoured more
Of him who rules above; so was his will
Pronounced among the gods, and by an oath,
That shook Heaven's whole circumference,
    confirmed.
Thither let us bend all our thoughts, to learn
355 What creatures there inhabit, of what mould,
Or substance, how endued, and what their power,
And where their weakness, how attempted best,
By force or subtlety. Though Heaven be shut,
And Heaven's high Arbitrator sit secure
360 In his own strength, this place may lie exposed
The utmost border of his kingdom, left
To their defence who hold it: here perhaps
Some advantageous act may be achieved
By sudden onset, either with Hell fire
365 To waste his whole creation, or possess
All as our own, and drive as we were driven,
The puny habitants, or if not drive,
Seduce them to our party, that their God
May prove their foe, and with repenting hand
370 Abolish his own works. This would surpass
Common revenge, and interrupt his joy
In our confusion, and our joy upraise
In his disturbance; when his darling sons
Hurled headlong to partake with us, shall curse
375 Their frail originals and faded bliss,
Faded so soon. Advise if this be worth
Attempting, or to sit in darkness here

Hatching vain empires?' Thus Beëlzebub
Pleaded his devilish counsel, first devised
380 By Satan, and in part proposed: for whence,
But from the author of all ill could spring
So deep a malice, to confound the race
Of Mankind in one root, and Earth with Hell
To mingle and involve, done all to spite
385 The great Creator? But their spite still serves
His glory to augment. The bold design
Pleased highly those infernal states, and joy
Sparkled in all their eyes; with full assent
They vote: whereat his speech he thus renews.

390 **Beëlzebub:** 'Well have ye judged, well ended long debate,
Synod of gods, and like to what ye are,
Great things resolved; which from the lowest deep
Will once more lift us up, in spite of fate,
Nearer our ancient seat; perhaps in view
395 Of those bright confines, whence with neighbouring arms
And opportune excursion we may chance
Re-enter Heaven; or else in some mild zone
Dwell not unvisited of Heaven's fair light
Secure, and at the brightening orient beam
400 Purge off this gloom; the soft delicious air,
To heal the scar of these corrosive fires
Shall breathe her balm. But first whom shall we send
In search of this new world, whom shall we find
Sufficient? who shall tempt with wandering feet
405 The dark unbottomed infinite abyss
And through the palpable obscure find out
His uncouth way, or spread his airy flight
Upborne with indefatigable wings
Over the vast abrupt, ere he arrive
410 The happy isle; what strength, what art can then
Suffice, or what evasion bear him safe

Through the strict sentries and stations thick
Of angels watching round? Here he had need
All circumspection, and we now no less
415   Choice in our suffrage; for on whom we send,
The weight of all and our last hope relies.'
    This said, he sat; and expectation held
His look suspense, awaiting who appeared
To second, or oppose, or undertake
420   The perilous attempt: but all sat mute,
Pondering the danger with deep thoughts; and each
In other's countenance read his own dismay
Astonished: none among the choice and prime
Of those Heaven-warring champions could be found
425   So hardy as to proffer or accept
Alone the dreadful voyage; till at last
Satan, whom now transcendent glory raised
Above his fellows, with monarchal pride
Conscious of highest worth, unmoved thus spake.

430 **Satan:** 'O progeny of heaven, empyreal thrones,
With reason hath deep silence and demur
Seized us, though undismayed: long is the way
And hard, that out of Hell leads up to light;
Our prison strong, this huge convex of fire,
435   Outrageous to devour, immures us round
Ninefold, and gates of burning adamant
Barred over us prohibit all egress.
These passed, if any pass, the void profound
Of unessential night receives him next
440   Wide gaping, and with utter loss of being
Threatens him, plunged in that abortive gulf.
If thence he scape into whatever world,
Or unknown region, what remains him less,
Than unknown dangers and as hard escape?
445   But I should ill become this throne, O peers,

And this imperial sovereignty, adorned
With splendour, armed with power, if aught proposed
And judged of public moment, in the shape
Of difficulty or danger could deter
450   Me from attempting. Wherefore do I assume
These royalties, and not refuse to reign,
Refusing to accept as great a share
Of hazard as of honour, due alike
To him who reigns, and so much to him due
455   Of hazard more, as he above the rest
High honoured sits? Go therefore mighty powers,
Terror of Heaven, though fallen; intend at home,
While here shall be our home, what best may ease
The present misery, and render Hell
460   More tolerable; if there be cure or charm
To respite or deceive, or slack the pain
Of this ill mansion: intermit no watch
Against a wakeful foe, while I abroad
Through all the coasts of dark destruction seek
465   Deliverance for us all: this enterprise
None shall partake with me.'

                              Thus saying rose
The monarch, and prevented all reply,
Prudent, lest from his resolution raised
Others among the chief might offer now
470   (Certain to be refused) what erst they feared;
And so refused might in opinion stand
His rivals, winning cheap the high repute
Which he through hazard huge must earn. But they
Dreaded not more th'adventure than his voice
475   Forbidding; and at once with him they rose;
Their rising all at once was as the sound
Of thunder heard remote. Towards him they bend
With awful reverence prone; and as a god

Extol him equal to the highest in Heaven:
480 Nor failed they to express how much they praised,
That for the general safety he despised
His own: for neither do the spirits damned
Lose all their virtue; lest bad men should boast
Their specious deeds on earth, which glory excites,
485 Or close ambition varnished o'er with zeal.
Thus they their doubtful consultations dark
Ended rejoicing in their matchless chief:
As when from mountain tops the dusky clouds
Ascending, while the north wind sleeps, o'erspread
490 Heaven's cheerful face, the louring element
Scowls o'er the darkened landskip snow, or shower;
If chance the radiant sun with farewell sweet
Extend his evening beam, the fields revive,
The birds their notes renew, and bleating herds
495 Attest their joy, that hill and valley rings.
O shame to men! Devil with devil damned
Firm concord holds, men only disagree
Of creatures rational, though under hope
Of heavenly grace: and God proclaiming peace,
500 Yet live in hatred, enmity, and strife
Among themselves, and levy cruel wars,
Wasting the earth, each other to destroy:
As if (which might induce us to accord)
Man had not hellish foes enow besides,
505 That day and night for his destruction wait.

The Stygian council thus dissolved; and forth
In order came the grand infernal peers,
Midst came their mighty paramount, and seemed
Alone the antagonist of Heaven, nor less
510 Than Hell's dread emperor with pomp supreme,
And God-like imitated state; him round
A globe of fiery seraphim enclosed

With bright emblazonry, and horrent arms.
Then of their session ended they bid cry
515 With trumpets' regal sound the great result:
Toward the four winds four speedy cherubim
Put to their mouths the sounding alchemy
By herald's voice explained: the hollow abyss
Heard far and wide, and all the host of Hell
520 With deafening shout returned them loud acclaim.
Thence more at ease their minds and somewhat raised
By false presumptuous hope, the rangèd powers
Disband, and wandering, each his several way
Pursues, as inclination or sad choice
525 Leads him perplexed, where he may likeliest find
Truce to his restless thoughts, and entertain
The irksome hours, till his great chief return.
Part on the plain, or in the air sublime
Upon the wing, or in swift race contend,
530 As at th'Olympian games or Pythian fields;
Part curb their fiery steeds, or shun the goal
With rapid wheels, or fronted brigads form.
As when to warn proud cities war appears
Waged in the troubled sky, and armies rush
535 To battle in the clouds, before each van
Prick forth the airy knights, and couch their spears
Till thickest legions close; with feats of arms
From either end of heaven the welkin burns.
Others with vast Typhœan rage more fell
540 Rend up both rocks and hills, and ride the air
In whirlwind; Hell scarce holds the wild uproar.
As when Alcides from Oechalia crowned
With conquest, felt th'envenomed robe, and tore
Through pain up by the roots Thessalian pines,
545 And Lichas from the top of Oeta threw
Into the Euboic sea. Others more mild,
Retreated in a silent valley, sing

With notes angelical to many a harp
Their own heroic deeds and hapless fall
550   By doom of battle; and complain that fate
Free virtue should enthral to force or chance.
Their song was partial, but the harmony
(What could it less when spirits immortal sing?)
Suspended Hell, and took with ravishment
555   The thronging audience. In discóurse more sweet
(For eloquence the soul, song charms the sense)
Others apart sat on a hill retired,
In thoughts more elevate, and reasoned high
Of providence, foreknowledge, will, and fate,
560   Fixed fate, free will, foreknowledge absolute,
And found no end, in wandering mazes lost.
Of good and evil much they argued then,
Of happiness and final misery,
Passion and apathy, and glory and shame,
565   Vain wisdom all, and false philosophy:
Yet with a pleasing sorcery could charm
Pain for a while or anguish, and excite
Fallacious hope, or arm th'obdurèd breast
With stubborn patience as with triple steel.

570   Another part in squadrons and gross bands,
On bold adventure to discover wide
That dismal world, if any clime perhaps
Might yield them easier habitation, bend
Four ways their flying march, along the banks
575   Of four infernal rivers that disgorge
Into the burning lake their baleful streams;
Abhorrèd Styx the flood of deadly hate,
Sad Acheron of sorrow, black and deep;
Cocytus, named of lamentation loud
580   Heard on the rueful stream; fierce Phlegethon
Whose waves of torrent fire inflame with rage.

Far off from these a slow and silent stream,
Lethè the river of oblivion rolls
Her watery labyrinth, whereof who drinks,
585   Forthwith his former state and being forgets,
Forgets both joy and grief, pleasure and pain.
Beyond this flood a frozen continent
Lies dark and wild, beat with perpetual storms
Of whirlwind and dire hail, which on firm land
590   Thaws not, but gathers heap, and ruin seems
Of ancient pile; all else deep snow and ice,
A gulf profound as that Serbonian bog
Betwixt Damiata and Mount Casius old,
Where armies whole have sunk: the parching air
595   Burns frore, and cold performs th'effect of fire.
Thither by harpy-footed Furies haled,
At certain revolutions all the damned
Are brought: and feel by turns the bitter change
Of fierce extremes, extremes by change more fierce,
600   From beds of raging fire to starve in ice
Their soft ethereal warmth, and there to pine
Immovable, infixed, and frozen round,
Periods of time, thence hurried back to fire.
They ferry over this Lethean sound
605   Both to and fro, their sorrow to augment,
And wish and struggle, as they pass, to reach
The tempting stream, with one small drop to lose
In sweet forgetfulness all pain and woe,
All in one moment, and so near the brink;
610   But fate withstands, and to oppose th'attempt
Medusa with Gorgonian terror guards
The ford, and of itself the water flies
All taste of living wight, as once it fled
The lip of Tantalus. Thus roving on
615   In confused march forlorn, th'adventurous bands
With shuddering horror pale, and eyes aghast

Viewed first their lámentable lot, and found
No rest: through many a dark and dreary vale
They passed, and many a region dolorous,
620 O'er many a frozen, many a fiery alp,
Rocks, caves, lakes, fens, bogs, dens, and shades of
   death,
A universe of death, which God by curse
Created evil, for evil only good,
Where all life dies, death lives, and nature breeds,
625 Perverse, all monstrous, all prodigious things,
Abominable, inutterable, and worse
Than fables yet have feigned, or fear conceived,
Gorgons and Hydras, and Chimèras dire.

  Meanwhile the adversary of God and Man,
630 Satan with thoughts inflamed of highest design,
Puts on swift wings, and towards the gates of Hell
Explores his solitary flight; sometimes
He scours the right hand coast, sometimes the left,
Now shaves with level wing the deep, then soars
635 Up to the fiery concave touring high.
As when far off at sea a fleet descried
Hangs in the clouds, by equinoctial winds
Close sailing from Bengala, or the isles
Of Ternate and Tidore, whence merchants bring
640 Their spicy drugs: they on the trading flood
Through the wide Ethiopian to the Cape
Ply stemming nightly toward the pole. So seemed
Far off the flying fiend: at last appear
Hell bounds high reaching to the horrid roof,
645 And thrice threefold the gates; three folds were brass,
Three irön, three of adamantine rock,
Impenetrable, impaled with circling fire,
Yet unconsumed. Before the gates there sat
On either side a formidable shape;

650   The one seemed woman to the waist, and fair,
           But ended foul in many a scaly fold
           Voluminous and vast, a serpent armed
           With mortal sting: about her middle round
           A cry of Hell hounds never ceasing barked
655   With wide Cerberean mouths full loud, and rung
           A hideous peal: yet, when they list, would creep,
           If aught disturbed their noise, into her womb,
           And kennel there, yet there still barked and howled
           Within unseen. Far less abhorred than these
660   Vexed Scylla bathing in the sea that parts
           Calabria from the hoarse Trinacrian shore:
           Nor uglier follow the night-hag, when called
           In secret, riding through the air she comes
           Lured with the smell of infant blood, to dance
665   With Lapland witches, while the labouring moon
           Eclipses at their charms. The other shape,
           If shape it might be called that shape had none
           Distinguishable in member, joint, or limb,
           Or substance might be called that shadow seemed,
670   For each seemed either; black it stood as night,
           Fierce as ten Furies, terrible as Hell,
           And shook a dreadful dart; what seemed his head
           The likeness of a kingly crown had on.
           Satan was now at hand, and from his seat
675   The monster moving onwards came as fast
           With horrid strides, Hell trembled as he strode.
           Th'undaunted fiend what this might be admired,
           Admired, not feared; God and his Son except,
           Created thing nought valued he nor shunned;
680   And with disdainful look thus first began.

    Satan: 'Whence and what art thou, execrable shape,
           That dar'st, though grim and terrible, advance
           Thy miscreated front athwart my way

To yonder gates? through them I mean to pass,
685 That be assured, without leave asked of thee:
Retire, or taste thy folly, and learn by proof,
Hell-born, not to contend with spirits of Heaven.'
To whom the goblin full of wrath replied,
Death: 'Art thou that traitor angel, art thou he,
690 Who first broke peace in Heaven and faith, till then
Unbroken, and in proud rebellious arms
Drew after him the third part of Heaven's sons
Conjured against the Highest, for which both thou
And they outcast from God, are here condemned
695 To waste eternal days in woe and pain?
And reckon'st thou thyself with spirits of Heaven,
Hell-doomed, and breath'st defiance here and scorn
Where I reign king, and to enrage thee more,
Thy king and lord? Back to thy punishment,
700 False fugitive, and to thy speed add wings,
Lest with a whip of scorpions I pursue
Thy lingering, or with one stroke of this dart
Strange horror seize thee, and pangs unfelt before.'
So spake the grisly terror, and in shape,
705 So speaking and so threatening, grew tenfold
More dreadful and deform: on th'other side
Incensed with indignation Satan stood
Unterrified, and like a comet burned,
That fires the length of Ophiucus huge
710 In th'arctic sky, and from his horrid hair
Shakes pestilence and war. Each at the head
Levelled his deadly aim; their fatal hands
No second stroke intend, and such a frown
Each cast at th'other, as when two black clouds
715 With heaven's artillery fraught, come rattling on
Over the Caspian, then stand front to front
Hovering a space, till winds the signal blow
To join their dark encounter in mid air:

So frowned the mighty combatants, that Hell
720 Grew darker at their frown, so matched they stood;
For never but once more was either like
To meet so great a foe: and now great deeds
Had been achieved, whereof all Hell had rung,
Had not the snaky sorceress that sat
725 Fast by Hell gate, and kept the fatal key,
Risen, and with hideous outcry rushed between.
Sin: 'O father, what intends thy hand,' she cried,
'Against thy only son? What fury, O son,
Possesses thee to bend that mortal dart
730 Against thy father's head? and know'st for whom?
For him who sits above and laughs the while
At thee ordained his drudge, to execute
Whate'er his wrath, which he calls justice, bids,
His wrath which one day will destroy ye both.'
735 She spake, and at her words the hellish pest
Forbore, then these to her Satan returned:
Satan: 'So strange thy outcry, and thy words so strange
Thou interposest, that my sudden hand
Prevented spares to tell thee yet by deeds
740 What it intends; till first I know of thee,
What thing thou art, thus double-formed, and why
In this infernal vale first met thou call'st
Me father, and that phantasm call'st my son?
I know thee not, nor ever saw till now
745 Sight more detestable than him and thee.'

T'whom thus the portress of Hell gate replied:
Sin: 'Hast thou forgot me then, and do I seem
Now in thine eye so foul, once deemed so fair
In Heaven, when at the assembly, and in sight
750 Of all the seraphim with thee combined
In bold conspiracy against Heaven's King,
All on a sudden miserable pain

Surprised thee, dim thine eyes, and dizzy swum
In darkness, while thy head flames thick and fast
755 Threw forth, till on the left side opening wide,
Likest to thee in shape and countenance bright,
Then shining heavenly fair, a goddess armed
Out of thy head I sprung: amazement seized
All th'host of Heaven; back they recoiled afraid
760 At first, and called me Sin, and for a sign
Portentous held me; but familiar grown,
I pleased, and with attractive graces won
The most averse, thee chiefly, who full oft
Thyself in me thy perfect image viewing
765 Becam'st enamoured, and such joy thou took'st
With me in secret, that my womb conceived
A growing burden. Meanwhile war arose,
And fields were fought in heaven; wherein remained
(For what could else) to our almighty Foe
770 Clear victory, to our part loss and rout
Through all th'Empyrean: down they fell
Driven headlong from the pitch of Heaven, down
Into this deep, and in the general fall
I also; at which time this powerful key
775 Into my hand was given, with charge to keep
These gates for ever shut, which none can pass
Without my opening. Pensive here I sat
Alone, but long I sat not, till my womb
Pregnant by thee, and now excessive grown
780 Prodigious motion felt and rueful throes.
At last this odious offspring whom thou seest
Thine own begotten, breaking violent way
Tore through my entrails, that with fear and pain
Distorted, all my nether shape thus grew
785 Transformed: but he my inbred enemy
Forth issued, brandishing his fatal dart
Made to destroy: I fled, and cried out 'Death';

Hell trembled at the hideous name, and sighed
From all her caves, and back resounded 'Death'.
790   I fled, but he pursued (though more, it seems,
Inflamed with lust than rage) and swifter far,
Me overtook his mother all dismayed,
And in embraces forcible and foul
Ingendering with me, of that rape begot
795   These yelling monsters that with ceaseless cry
Surround me, as thou saw'st, hourly conceived
And hourly born, with sorrow infinite
To me, for when they list into the womb
That bred them they return, and howl and gnaw
800   My bowels, their repast; then bursting forth
Afresh with conscious terrors vex me round,
That rest or intermission none I find.
Before mine eyes in opposition sits
Grim Death my son and foe, who sets them on,
805   And me his parent would full soon devour
For want of other prey, but that he knows
His end with mine involved; and knows that I
Should prove a bitter morsel, and his bane,
Whenever that shall be; so fate pronounced.
810   But thou, O father, I forewarn thee, shun
His deadly arrow; neither vainly hope
To be invulnerable in those bright arms,
Though tempered heavenly, for that mortal dint,
Save he who reigns above, none can resist.'

815   She finished, and the subtle fiend his lore
Soon learned, now milder, and thus answered smooth.
Satan: 'Dear daughter, since thou claim'st me for thy sire,
And my fair son here show'st me, the dear pledge
Of dalliance had with thee in Heaven, and joys
820   Then sweet, now sad to mention, through dire change
Befallen us unforeseen, unthought of, know

I come no enemy, but to set free
From out this dark and dismal house of pain,
Both him and thee, and all the heavenly host
825   Of spirits that in our just pretences armed
Fell with us from on high: from them I go
This uncouth errand sole, and one for all
Myself expose, with lonely steps to tread
Th'unfounded deep, and through the void immense
830   To search with wandering quest a place foretold
Should be, and, by concurring signs, ere now
Created vast and round, a place of bliss
In the purlieus of Heaven, and therein placed
A race of upstart creatures, to supply
835   Perhaps our vacant room, though more removed,
Lest Heaven surcharged with potent multitude
Might hap to move new broils. Be this or aught
Than this more secret now designed, I haste
To know, and this once known, shall soon return,
840   And bring ye to the place where thou and Death
Shall dwell at ease, and up and down unseen
Wing silently the buxom air, embalmed
With odours; there ye shall be fed and filled
Immeasurably, all things shall be your prey.'
845   He ceased, for both seemed highly pleased, and Death
Grinned horrible a ghastly smile, to hear
His famine should be filled, and blessed his maw
Destined to that good hour: no less rejoiced
His mother bad, and thus bespake her sire.
850 **Sin:** 'The key of this infernal pit by due,
And by command of Heaven's all-powerful King
I keep, by him forbidden to unlock
These adamantine gates; against all force
Death ready stands to interpose his dart,
855   Fearless to be o'ermatched by living might.
But what owe I to his commands above

Who hates me, and hath hither thrust me down
Into this gloom of Tartarus profound,
To sit in hateful office here confined,
860   Inhabitant of Heaven, and heavenly-born,
Here in perpetual agony and pain,
With terrors and with clamours compassed round
Of mine own brood, that on my bowels feed?
Thou art my father, thou my author, thou
865   My being gav'st me; whom should I obey
But thee, whom follow? thou wilt bring me soon
To that new world of light and bliss, among
The gods who live at ease, where I shall reign
At thy right hand voluptuous, as beseems
870   Thy daughter and thy darling, without end.'
    Thus saying, from her side the fatal key,
Sad instrument of all our woe, she took;
And towards the gate rolling her bestial train,
Forthwith the huge portcullis high updrew,
875   Which but herself not all the Stygian powers
Could once have moved; then in the key-hole turns
The intricate wards, and every bolt and bar
Of massy iron or solid rock with ease
Unfastens: on a sudden open fly
880   With impetuous recoil and jarring sound
The infernal doors, and on their hinges grate
Harsh thunder, that the lowest bottom shook
Of Érebus. She opened, but to shut
Excelled her power; the gates wide open stood,
885   That with extended wings a bannered host
Under spread ensigns marching might pass through
With horse and chariots ranked in loose array;
So wide they stood, and like a furnace mouth
Cast forth redounding smoke and ruddy flame.

890   Before their eyes in sudden view appear

The secrets of the hoary deep, a dark
Illimitable ocean without bound,
Without dimension, where length, breadth, and highth,
And time and place are lost; where eldest Night
895   And Chaos, ancestors of Nature, hold
Eternal anarchy, amidst the noise
Of endless wars, and by confusion stand.
For hot, cold, moist, and dry, four champions fierce
Strive here for mastery, and to battle bring
900   Their embryon atoms; they around the flag
Of each his faction, in their several clans,
Light-armed or heavy, sharp, smooth, swift or slow,
Swarm populous, unnumbered as the sands
Of Barca or Cyrenè's torrid soil,
905   Levied to side with warring winds, and poise
Their lighter wings. To whom these most adhere,
He rules a moment; Chaos umpire sits,
And by decision more embroils the fray
By which he reigns: next him high arbiter
910   Chance governs all. Into this wild abyss,
The womb of Nature and perhaps her grave,
Of neither sea, nor shore, nor air, nor fire,
But all these in their pregnant causes mixed
Confusedly, and which thus must ever fight,
915   Unless th'Almighty Maker them ordain
His dark materials to create more worlds,
Into this wild abyss the wary fiend
Stood on the brink of Hell and looked a while,
Pondering his voyage; for no narrow frith
920   He had to cross. Nor was his ear less pealed
With noises loud and ruinous (to compare
Great things with small) than when Bellona storms,
With all her battering engines bent to rase
Some capital city; or less than if this frame
925   Of heaven were falling, and these elements

In mutiny had from her axle torn
The steadfast Earth. At last his sail-broad vans
He spreads for flight, and in the surging smoke
Uplifted spurns the ground, thence many a league
930   As in a cloudy chair ascending rides
Audacious, but that seat soon failing, meets
A vast vacuity: all unawares
Flutt'ring his pennons vain plumb down he drops
Ten thousand fathom deep, and to this hour
935   Down had been falling, had not by ill chance
The strong rebuff of some tumultuous cloud
Instinct with fire and nitre hurried him
As many miles aloft: that fury stayed,
Quenched in a boggy Syrtis, neither sea,
940   Nor good dry land: nigh foundered on he fares,
Treading the crude consistence, half on foot,
Half flying; behoves him now both oar and sail.
As when a gryphon through the wilderness
With wingèd course o'er hill or moory dale,
945   Pursues the Arimaspian, who by stealth
Had from his wakeful custody purloined
The guarded gold: so eagerly the fiend
O'er bog or steep, through strait, rough, dense, or rare,
With head, hands, wings, or feet pursues his way,
950   And swims or sinks, or wades, or creeps, or flies.

At length a universal hubbub wild
Of stunning sounds and voices all confused
Borne through the hollow dark assaults his ear
With loudest vehemence: thither he plies,
955   Undaunted to meet there whatever power
Or spirit of the nethermost abyss
Might in that noise reside, of whom to ask
Which way the nearest coast of darkness lies
Bordering on light; when straight behold the throne

960   Of Chaos, and his dark pavilion spread
         Wide on the wasteful deep; with him enthroned
         Sat sable-vested Night, eldest of things,
         The consort of his reign; and by them stood
         Orcus and Adès, and the dreaded name
965   Of Demogorgon; Rumour next and Chance,
         And Tumult and Confusion all embroiled,
         And Discord with a thousand various mouths.
         T'whom Satan turning boldly, thus.

Satan: 'Ye powers
         And spirits of this nethermost abyss,
970   Chaos and ancient Night, I come no spy,
         With purpose to explore or to disturb
         The secrets of your realm, but by constraint
         Wandering this darksome desert, as my way
         Lies through your spacious empire up to light,
975   Alone, and without guide, half lost, I seek
         What readiest path leads where your gloomy bounds
         Confine with Heaven; or if some other place
         From your dominion won, th'ethereal King
         Possesses lately, thither to arrive
980   I travel this profound, direct my course;
         Directed no mean recompense it brings
         To your behoof, if I that region lost,
         All usurpation thence expelled, reduce
         To her original darkness and your sway
985   (Which is my present journey) and once more
         Erect the standard there of ancient Night.
         Yours be th'advantage all, mine the revenge.'
           Thus Satan; and him thus the anarch old
         With faltering speech and visage incomposed
990   Answered.

Chaos: 'I know thee, stranger, who thou art,
         That mighty leading angel, who of late
         Made head against Heaven's King, though overthrown.

I saw and heard, for such a numerous host
Fled not in silence through the frighted deep
995   With ruin upon ruin, rout on rout,
Confusion worse confounded; and Heaven gates
Poured out by millions her victorious bands
Pursuing. I upon my frontiers here
Keep residence; if all I can will serve,
1000   That little which is left so to defend,
Encroached on still through our intestine broils
Weakening the sceptre of old Night: first Hell
Your dungeon stretching far and wide beneath;
Now lately heaven and earth, another world
1005   Hung o'er my realm, linked in a golden chain
To that side Heaven from whence your legions fell:
If that way be your walk, you have not far;
So much the nearer danger; go and speed;
Havoc and spoil and ruin are my gain.'

1010   He ceased; and Satan stayed not to reply,
But glad that now his sea should find a shore,
With fresh alacrity and force renewed
Springs upward like a pyramid of fire
Into the wild expanse, and through the shock
1015   Of fighting elements, on all sides round
Environed wins his way; harder beset
And more endangered, than when Argo passed
Through Bosphorus, betwixt the justling rocks:
Or when Ulýsses on the larboard shunned
1020   Charybdis, and by th'other whirlpool steered.
So he with difficulty and labour hard
Moved on, with difficulty and labour he;
But he once past, soon after when Man fell,
Strange alteration! Sin and Death amain
1025   Following his track, such was the will of Heaven,
Paved after him a broad and beaten way

Over the dark abyss, whose boiling gulf
Tamely endured a bridge of wondrous length
From hell continued reaching the utmost orb
1030 Of this frail world; by which the spirits perverse
With easy intercourse pass to and fro
To tempt or punish mortals, except whom
God and good angels guard by special grace.
But now at last the sacred influence
1035 Of light appears, and from the walls of Heaven
Shoots far into the bosom of dim night
A glimmering dawn; here nature first begins
Her farthest verge, and Chaos to retire
As from her outmost works a broken foe
1040 With tumult less and with less hostile din,
That Satan with less toil, and now with ease
Wafts on the calmer wave by dubious light
And like a weather-beaten vessel holds
Gladly the port, though shrouds and tackle torn;
1045 Or in the emptier waste, resembling air,
Weighs his spread wings, at leisure to behold
Far off th'empyreal Heaven, extended wide
In circuit, undetermined square or round,
With opal towers and battlements adorned
1050 Of living sapphire, once his native seat;
And fast by hanging in a golden chain
This pendent world, in bigness as a star
Of smallest magnitude close by the moon.
Thither full fraught with mischievous revenge,
1055 Accursed, and in a cursèd hour he hies.

Notes to Book 1

The Argument to Book 1

After he had published the first edition (the edition used in this book), Milton wrote an *Argument* or synopsis of events to place at the beginning of each book in the second edition of 1674. In the Argument to Book 1, Milton places the book in the context of the theme of the whole poem (*Man's disobedience, and the loss thereupon of Paradise*), its timescale (*the midst of things*), and its geography (*a place of utter darkness*). He also outlines the events of Book 1, focusing on Satan's pivotal role in arousing his legions and preparing them for the next stage in his battle against God.

7	**the midst of things**	the poem begins *in media res*, in the middle of the story, as a Greek epic does.
9	**heaven and earth**	the sky and the earth (not God's Heaven).
10–11	**fitliest called Chaos**	Hell is in the middle of Chaos; see the illustration on page 11.
13, 15	**confusion, confounded**	these words suggest their Latin etymology (*confusi*: poured out; *confundi*: thrown down).
13	**him who next in order**	i.e. Beelzebub.
16	**named**	are named.
22	**ancient Fathers**	theologians of the early Catholic Church (such as St Augustine, who argued that the angels were made long before the visible creation of the world, so that Milton must suggest that Satan only knew about this from a prophecy).
23	**determine**	decide.
23–4	**What his associates thence attempt**	i.e. the building of Pandæmonium.

Milton's invocation: Lines 1–26

Milton starts his poem as Homer started the classical epic, the *Iliad* some 2000 years before (see Interpretations pages 149–50), by addressing ('invoking') a Muse, a goddess personifying artistic inspiration. Milton distinguishes his as the true *heavenly Muse* who had dictated the Bible (which he sees as a kind of sacred poetry) to Moses and its other 'authors'. Milton sees himself as a second Moses, inspired by this exalted Muse to make his poem far surpass classical epic in the grandeur of its theme. The first 16 lines are analysed in Interpretations page 156.

2   **mortal**   deadly.

4   **Eden**   the garden of Eden or Paradise, from where Adam and Eve were driven after they had eaten the fruit of the forbidden tree.

     one greater Man   Christ, who restored us to the blissful seat of Heaven when he paid for this first sin by dying on the Cross (see page 13).

6   **heavenly Muse**   see headnote above.

7   **Oreb… Sinai**   places where the *shepherd* Moses is said to have seen God (Exodus 3, 19), so being inspired to write Genesis, which describes the beginning of the world. (For Bible text used in Notes, see Appendix page 196).

10–11   **Sion hill… Siloa's brook**   places which inspired New Testament writers; Jesus (the *oracle of God*) taught at Sion (where the Temple stood) and cured a blind man close to (*fast by*) Siloa (John 9).

15   **th'Aonian mount**   Helicon, the mountain sacred to the Muses (see headnote).

18   **th'upright heart and pure**   the Holy Spirit lives within the temple of the body.

19   **Instruct**   main verb which, like *Sing* (6), *Moved* (29), and *Stirred* (35), is frequently placed at the beginning of the line.

21   **Dove-like**   in Genesis the creative 'spirit of God moved upon the face of the waters', and the dove showed Noah that the flood was over (Genesis 1 and 8).

     brooding   meditating, but also sitting like a hen on her eggs; Milton may be alluding to the ancient idea that the world was born from an egg.

22–3 **what in me is dark/Illumine** perhaps a reference to Milton's own blindness, which also introduces his constant identification of God with light and upward movement (see Interpretations pages 165–6).

25–6 This is the purpose of the whole poem: to explain God's Providence, or care and plan for humanity, which underlies the often painful *ways of God*.

The scope of the whole poem: Lines 27–49

Milton now gives a brief synopsis of the story of the whole poem (see pages 9–12). First, he tells us what is to come after the events of Books 1 and 2: the corruption of Adam and Eve in the garden of Eden by Satan, disguised as a *serpent* (see Genesis 3). Then he briefly explains Satan's motivation: *envy* of humankind's happiness, and *revenge* against God for having thrown him and his angel-supporters out of Heaven. They were punished in this way because he had led them in a rebellion against God which resulted in a war in Heaven (see page 12). Note the focus on *Man's first disobedience* (1:1); Satan is only introduced because Milton wants to explain how evil entered the world.

28 **Nor** not even.

29 **grandparents** Adam and Eve, from whom the whole human species was believed to be descended.

30–1 **fall off, transgress** desert, disobey.

32 Because of a single restriction (on tasting one fruit); otherwise they had command of the Earth.

33 **seduced** tempted to corruption.

34 **Th'infernal serpent** Satan, who was the immediate *cause* (28) of Adam and Eve's eating the fruit (their *revolt*), disguised as a serpent. Note the qualities here ascribed to Satan (see Interpretations pages 172–3).

36 **the mother of Mankind** Eve.
what time at the time when.

37 **host** army.

38–41 Satan had previously been an angel in Heaven who tried to become supreme over other angels (*his peers*), and, using his own host of *rebel angels*, believed (*trusted*) he could *oppose* and defeat *the most High* God himself (see page 12).

43   **Raised**   stirred up (main verb).

44   **vain**   unsuccessful.

     Him   Satan, object of *Hurled* (see Interpretations page 155).

45   **th'ethereal**   heavenly (highest part of atmosphere).

46   **ruin**   falling (see Luke 10:18: 'I beheld Satan as lightning fall from Heaven').

47   **perdition**   loss.

48   **adamantine**   fabulous unbreakable mineral (see Jude 1:6 in the Bible).

The description of Hell: Lines 50–83

Milton describes Hell in the Argument as *a place of utter darkness*, meaning 'outer' as well as complete, and suggesting the furthest distance a creature can travel away from God (see page 14). For a discussion on Milton's stylistic devices for conveying this half-real, half-abstract setting, and his implication that it can exist within the human mind, see pages 166–7 and 175. It is illuminating to compare it with *Prometheus Bound*; see page 170 and Appendix page 197.

50   **Nine times**   the rebel angels fell for nine days (6:871) like the Titans, to whom they are frequently compared (see note to 1:197–200); they are then chained for nine days on the burning lake, a punishment suggested by Revelation 20:10.

51   **horrid**   causing horror but also bristling, shaggy (because it is associated with hair standing up; one of Milton's favourite words).

53   **Confounded though immortal**   cast down although unable to die. The fallen angels are made of immortal fire (see page 14), but since they sinned they can be cast down and in pain.

53–4   **doom/Reserved**   the judgement (*doom*) on him had preserved him to suffer more of God's wrath.

56–7   **his baleful eyes/That witnessed**   his eyes, both evil and in pain, expressed and saw the disaster.

59   **ken**   range of vision or knowledge.

64   **discover**   reveal.

65   **doleful**   sorrowful. Note the way the scenery suggests emotions (see Interpretations pages 166–7).

66–7   **hope never comes/That comes to all**   perhaps echoing the
        words inscribed above the gate of Dante's Hell: 'All hope abandon
        ye who enter here'; see Interpretations page 150.

68   **urges**   drives on (the sense of the Latin *urgeo*).

69   **sulphur**   brimstone, a corrosive chemical traditionally associated
        with Hell, which burns here without being used up (*unconsumed*).

71   **ordained**   ordered, prepared.

72   **portion**   place, fate.

73–4   The distance from Hell to Heaven is three times the distance from
        the centre of the Earth to the outermost orbit of the stars. See the
        illustration on page 11. As in line 50, Milton's calculations are
        based on the mystical number 3.

75   **unlike**   the fallen angels will try to make it more like Heaven; see
        headnote to 1:670–751, page 103.

78   **discerns**   makes out in the gloom.
        weltering   wallowing helplessly.

81   **Beëlzebub**   'Lord of the Flies', and called 'Prince of the Devils in
        Mark 3:22 (which is set in Palestine). He is Satan's second-in-
        command; see Interpretations page 177.
        arch-enemy   the supreme enemy. *Enemy* is the principal meaning
        of the name *Satan*, though Satan frequently tries to apply it to
        God (for example, 1:122).

Satan's first speech: Lines 84–126

These lines introduce us to two sides of Satan's character: is he the
noble and suffering hero standing firm against overwhelming odds, or
the deceitful politician disguising his failure from his closest friend?
See Interpretations pages 172–3. He is already taking control of the
angels' future, for he rejects some possible options (for example, 108,
111), and is only questioning whether to use *force or guile* (121) in his
continued war against God. This will be debated from 2:41. The main
points he makes are reinforced by Beëlzebub, and listed at the
headnote to 1:127–55, page 81. Make a list of the ways he
characterizes God (for example, *potent Victor in his rage* [95]); how far
do these names help him to excuse his own failure?

84–94   **If thou beest he...**   if you really are Beëlzebub, whom Satan says
        misery hath joined (main verb, 90) to him now, since God
        surprisingly proved stronger than them.

85–7 **who in the happy... though bright**   Satan used to be called Lucifer, 'light-bearer', and presumably Beëlzebub was nearly as bright in Heaven (*the happy realms of light*) if he shone brighter than the *Myriads* (vast numbers) there.

87 **if he whom mutual league**   if you are really he who once *joined* (90) in alliance with me (but was it really *mutual?*) to help each other in the *glorious enterprise* (89) to overthrow God.

92 **highth**   height. Milton's spelling intensifies the highness.

93 **thunder**   the *ten thousand thunders* of 6:836 with which Jesus cast out the rebel angels (described at 94 as *dire arms*).

94 **dire**   terrible.

94–105 **Yet not... shook his throne**   fear will not cause Satan to *repent or change* (main verbs, 96) the mind that fought against God, because his pride (*disdain*) and sense *of injured merit* (98) persists. Satan was provoked to rebel by God's promotion of Jesus over himself (5:662), and claims that his fellow rebels would have preferred him to the tyrants, God and Jesus; see page 12.

95 **potent**   powerful.

99–100 **contend, contention**   oppose, opposition.

102 **durst**   dared to.

104 **dubious**   uncertain (but was it really uncertain?).

105 **field**   battle.

109 And what else cannot be overcome?

111–16 **To bow and sue... downfall**   Satan anticipates his soliloquy in Book 4 here (see Interpretations page 176) by saying it would indeed be ignoble to ask God for forgiveness on bended knee, since God (the *Who* of 113) had so recently been afraid of him.

112 **deify**   make divine (ironic, as God *is* divine).

115 **ignominy**   disgrace.

116–21 **since by fate... eternal war**   *fate* (a power Satan prefers to God, see Interpretations page 176) ensures that the angelic *substance* of *gods* (his name for the angels) cannot die, and as they will have improved in experience, so they may *with more successful hope* (120) continue the war with God, using either *force or guile*.

117 **empyreal substance**   the pure fire out of which the highest heaven is made; see page 14.

118 **event**   outcome.

119 Our weapons are no worse and our understanding of the possible outcome is much better.

122	**Foe**	see Note to 1:81.
124	**tyranny of Heaven**	see page 3 for political implications.
126	**Vaunting**	boasting. This line sums up Satan's two sides; see Interpretations page 173 on Satan's despair.

Beëlzebub's first speech: Lines 127–55

We discover here something of Beëlzebub's character and his relationship with Satan. See if you can find the following ideas expressed in both this speech and Satan's:

- a preference for seeing *fate* or *chance* as the supreme power
- the claim that God's victory was solely one of *strength*
- reliance on the immortality of their *heavenly essences*
- the belief that the mind can remain unchanged.

However, as Beëlzebub continues to speak, his view of the situation begins to differ from Satan's, particularly with regard to God's power. Can you see this happen? Once again it is worth listing the ways in which God is described.

128–42		Another very long and complex sentence; having addressed Satan for six lines, Beëlzebub reaches his main point at 134 (main verbs *see* and *rue*).
128	**thronèd powers**	rulers in the hierarchy of angels. Heaven is organized like an army (see page 12).
129	**th'embattled seraphim**	armed angels (the *seraphim* were the second highest rank).
130	**conduct**	leadership (Latin *duco* I lead).
132	**his**	God's.
134	**rue**	regret.
138	**heavenly essences**	another way of referring to the *empyreal substance* explained in the Note to 1:117.
140	**vigour**	physical strength. Beëlzebub here takes pride in their returning strength, but begins at 146 to wonder why it is returning. For the answer see Note to 210–13 below.
141	**glory extinct**	brightness has been extinguished (see line 97).
144	**Of force**	perforce, by necessity.
143–52		Beëlzebub is afraid that their returning strength will enable them to endure or *support* increased torture, or even to perform God's *errands* (as perhaps they will; see Note to 1:210–13 and

Interpretations page 177). What does this tell you about his attitude to God?

146   **entire**   undamaged.

148   **suffice his vengeful ire**   satisfy his wrathful and sadistic passion for revenge.

149–50   **thralls/By right of war**   contemporary prisoners of war could, in theory, be made the slaves (*thralls*) of the conquerors.

153   **avail**   benefit.

Satan's returning decision and freedom: Lines 156–91

Satan's reply begins to explain why and how he will continue his opposition to God. Lines 162–8 should be read in conjunction with 211–20, which states God's counter-policy (see page 13). What does Satan's policy suggest to you? Is it childish? spiteful? heroic in the face of overwhelming odds? What does it tell you about Satan's feeling for God?

157   **Fallen cherub**   Beëlzebub, whom Satan is addressing.

157–8   **weak is miserable/Doing or suffering**   this is one of a number of places where a contrast can be drawn between Satan and Christ, who did not despise weakness. *Doing/suffering* (or active/passive) represents the contrasting types of human behaviour; you can use this opposition to analyse the debate between the angels in Book 2: some want to *do* and some to *suffer* (see 2:199).

159   **aught**   anything.

162–8   God's caring plan for creation (his *Providence*), explained by Milton in 1:211–20, will indeed seek *Out of our evil... to bring forth good*. Satan plans to *pervert that end* by frustrating God wherever possible in order to *grieve him* and *disturb* his plans (*inmost counsels*).

169–70   **angry Victor**   God, as Satan presents him, for God is in fact mercifully calling back the angelic pursuers, who are therefore not acting as agents (*ministers*) of vengeance at all.

171–3   **sulphurous hail... o'erblown hath laid/The fiery surge**   the sulphur-rain that was *Shot after us* has blown itself out, so that the lake of fire (*fiery surge*) is now calm (*laid*). The weather is improving.

175–6　　This suggests a cartoon picture, in which the thunderbolts have lightning wings. Satan hopes it has run out of missiles (*spent his shafts*), thus concealing again the fact that God must be easing their torments on purpose.

176　　**his**　its (a relatively new word which Milton avoids).

177　　To resonate through Hell (the open vowels echo the meaning).

178　　**slip**　miss. What does this tell you of Satan's character?

178–9　　**scorn,/Or satiate fury**　Satan calls God's mercy *scorn* and suggests that his sadistic appetite is simply satisfied (*satiate*) for the moment.

180　　**dreary plain**　Satan chooses this plain, which is described in emotional as well as physical terms, as the assembly ground for his troops.

181　　**seat**　place.
　　　　void　empty.

182　　**Save**　except.
　　　　livid　bluish leaden colour.

183　　**Thither... tend**　let us go there.

185　　**rest**　Hell is characterized by change and restlessness; see Interpretations page 167.

187　　**Consult**　main verb at the beginning of a line. But is Satan really going to consult his fellow angels? What decisions must he already have made to be now consulting on the issues which are outlined here?

189　　**dire**　terrible.

190　　**reinforcement**　encouragement.

191　　**despair**　emphasized by rhyme with *repair* (188). Why is this passion so appropriate to Satan and to Hell, and how is it related to *hope* (190)?

First description of Satan: Lines 192–241

This passage includes the first **epic similes,** elaborate comparisons usually introduced by *As* and completed by *So*; see Interpretations pages 152–3. By looking at all the features which Satan has in common with the Titans, with Leviathan, or with a volcano, you can uncover what Milton is telling us about Satan apart from the fact that he is very big.

Milton also confronts here the central problem of why God allowed

Satan to exist at all, let alone to have his freedom (*Left him at large*, 213). The principal answer given here is that this policy would ultimately allow God to show a much greater *grace* when he redeems the world by the sacrifice of Christ, but see page 13 for a wider discussion.

193–5	**head up-lift... Prone**	head lifted up, body lying flat. What does this position suggest to you? Compare it with the next images of Satan rearing up and then flying to land (221, 225).
196	**rood**	rod, an ancient unit of measurement, equal to about five metres.
197–200	**As whom... Tarsus held**	*As* introduces the first epic simile, comparing Satan to *Titanian... Briareos or Typhon*, two giant-monsters of the Titan race; Briareos had 100 arms, Typhon (who lived at *Tarsus*) 100 heads. The Titans deposed their father-king (Uranus), and later their new king (Saturn) was himself deposed by his son, Zeus. See 1:508–14 and Interpretations page 149.
201	**Leviathan**	enormous biblical sea-monster generally identified with the whale, and to which Milton attaches the Scandinavian (and *Arabian Nights*) fairy tale of a monster as big as an island, which deceives sailors into mooring to its hide (*rind*, 206) before swimming away with them.
203–8		The sentence-structure goes: *The pilot* (subject) *Moors* (main verb at beginning of line) by *Him* (= Leviathan) while he is *slumbering* (203).
203	**haply**	by chance.
204	**night-foundered skiff**	a small boat disabled and leaking at night. Satan is often associated with night and the sea.
205	**Deeming**	believing.
207	**under the lea**	on the side sheltered from the wind.
208	**Invests**	clothes.
209	**So**	marks the end of these epic similes.
210–11	**nor ever thence/Had risen**	nor would ever have risen from there.
211–13	**but that... dark designs**	Milton here intrudes his own voice to answer Beëlzebub's question at 143–52 and Satan's boast at 162–68; Milton follows St Augustine in the belief that ultimately everything that happens is within God's plan or *Providence* (see page 13).
213	**at large**	at liberty.
214	**reiterated**	repeated.

216   **enraged**   filled with rage.

219   **On Man by him seduced**   God's *grace* will be shown to humankind because they were induced to commit sin (*seduced*) by Satan.

221   **Forthwith**   straight away.
       rears   raises, lifts (his *mighty stature*).

222–4   **on each hand... horrid vale**   Satan's sudden movement creates a trough bristling with fire (*horrid vale*) and surrounded by flames sloping away from it.

226   **incumbent**   leaning.

228   **He lights**   he alights, touches down, on the burning 'land' which surrounds the lake of fire.

230–7   This third epic simile appears to elaborate on Satan's *hue* (colour, 230) but is really a comparison of his movement with that of the torn mountainsides which Milton imagines would fly through the air when the Sicilian volcanoes *Pelorus* and *Etna* erupt. Milton had visited Sicily, but look for the words which suggest not eruption so much as an industrial explosion, or belching and farting demons (see the illustration on page 167).

231   **subterranean wind**   underground force (but why *wind?*).

233–5   **combustible... Sublimed**   the inflammable fuel in the centre of the mountain is ignited by the underground *wind* and immediately becomes flame and vapour.

236   **singèd bottom all involved**   the burnt floor, wrapped in *stench and smoke* (again note the body-related language) where the mountainside had been.

237   **such resting**   ironic, as there is no rest in Hell (see 1:66).

239   **glorying to have scaped**   triumphant in their escape.
       Stygian flood   hellish lake (alluding to the Greek Underworld river, the Styx).

241   **sufferance of supernal Power**   permission of almighty Power (referring to line 212 above).

Satan takes possession of his new kingdom: Lines 242–82

Here, as so often, Satan seems to see the truth only to manipulate it. How does he convey his sense of a real loss, but immediately excuse or justify himself, or in other ways change the facts? How far do you agree with Satan's assertion that *Here at least/We shall be free* (258–9)?

This is also one of several passages which 'internalize Hell' by suggesting it is essentially within the mind (see Interpretations pages 167 and 175). This exchange with Beëlzebub displays not only Satan's concern for his *associates and co-partners* (265), but also (according to the flattering Beëlzebub) his power over them. Do you think he is misusing it here?

242   **clime**   climate.

244–5   **gloom… light**   it shows that Satan is still partly good that he recognizes the essential superiority of light over darkness; Mammon confuses the distinction in 2:262–8.

246–7   **dispose and bid/What shall be right**   Satan asserts that God wilfully arranges and decides what is right (rather than acting righteously because he is good).

248   Satan claims equality with God in all but strength; compare 1:92, 133, 258.

253   **A mind not to be changed**   this is both heroic and deeply ironic; changelessness is an attribute of Heaven only, and Satan changes and deteriorates before our eyes; compare this speech with the spitefulness and lies of his thoughts in Book 2 (see Interpretations pages 172–4).

254–5   The truth that *The mind is its own place* explains how Satan could invent Sin in Heaven, and later suggests true hope for Adam, who is told he shall *possess/A Paradise within thee happier far* than the one he lost (12:586–7).

258   **thunder**   see Note to 1:93.

259   **free**   suggests the ideals of the Commonwealth; see page 4.

261   **we may reign secure**   how do you see the plural *we* here?

262   **worth ambition**   worth being ambitious for.

263   **Better to reign in Hell**   this sounds classically heroic; Caesar supposedly said 'I would rather be first in this miserable village than second in Rome' (Plutarch *Life* XI 2, or see Homer's *Odyssey* XI 489–91). But in a religious context it suggests a 'service to sin' (Romans 6) rather than the 'perfect freedom' of service to God (*Book of Common Prayer*). Mammon later describes what he thinks it would be like to *serve in Heaven*; see 2:237–43 and Interpretations page 168.

266   **astonished**   stunned.
       th'oblivious pool   they lie forgetful on the lake of fire (a transfered epithet).

267–9	**call them not… to try** follows *wherefore* of 264: 'why do we not call them to try once more?'
268	**mansion** dwelling (where they *manent*, from *manere* (Latin) meaning to remain).
269	**rallied arms** reassembled weapons.
273	Which none but the All-powerful could have prevented from winning.
274	**liveliest pledge** most vital promise. Beëlzebub claims that Satan's voice alone rallies the angels in tight corners (*worst extremes, perilous edge/Of battle, all assaults*, 276–7).
278	**resume** main verb, following *If* (274): 'they will become brave again'.
280	**yon** yonder.
281	**erewhile** previously.
282	**pernicious highth** deadly height.

Second description of Satan and his awakening of the fallen angels: Lines 283–330

This passage, with its classical and biblical epic similes (see Interpretations page 153 and the illustration on page 171) and its wonderful speech is one of the most heroic in the poem. Yet there may be other elements in the description of Satan and the angels, or in his address to them, which give you a more negative impression. Are the angels the victims of Satan's egotism, or are they being helped by him to recover their self-esteem and ability to act? The passage also introduces the story of the Flight from Egypt by Moses and the Jewish people, which is the source of many comparisons in Books 1 and 2.

283	**superior fiend** Satan now walks to the *shore* of the burning lake, from where he had flown to the *dreary plain* (180).
284–6	**ponderous shield… Behind him cast** he carried his weighty shield, hardened in heavenly fire (*Ethereal temper*), over his shoulder. Achilles, the hero of Homer's *Iliad*, has a similarly mighty shield which is described at length.
287–91	Epic simile introduced by *like* comparing the shield to the moon. Milton visited the then blind *Tuscan artist*, or astronomer, Galileo,

in Florence (situated in Valdarno in Tuscany) in 1638, and was probably allowed to view the moon through the telescope (*optic glass*), which Galileo was believed to have invented, from the nearby hill at *Fésolè* (Fiesole). This passage and Satan's associations with night and the moon are discussed in Interpretations page 154.

292–5   Compared to his spear, the tallest pine cut (*Hewn*) in Norway to be a mast for an *ammiral* (flagship) would have looked like a small stick (*wand* – no magical connotations). The size-shifting in these two similes is significant. The moon is bigger than the shield; the tree is smaller than the spear. It is as if Milton is using the telescope at both ends to create a dream-like effect.

296   **marl**   earth.

297   **azure**   blue.

297–8   **torrid clime... vaulted with fire**   Satan is painfully affected by the scorchingly hot climate under the fiery roof of Hell.

299   **Nathless**   nevertheless.

302   **as autumnal leaves**   the first of three epic similes for the fallen angels. They lie stunned (*entranced*, 301), as thick as the golden leaves on the valley floor at *Vallombrosa* (or 'valley of shadows') in Etruria or Tuscany. Vergil also compares the dead to fallen leaves; see Appendix page 198 and ask yourself whether the effect is the same in both. For Milton's enjoyment of names, see Interpretations page 160.

304   **scattered sedge**   the angels are thrown about like water-weed after a storm (associated with the appearance of the star-constellation *Orion*, who is *armed* with a sword, 305).

307   Pharaoh and the Egyptian troops (who drowned when Moses closed the waters of the Red Sea on them; Exodus 14).

308   **perfidious hatred**   treacherous hostility; the Egyptians, like Satan's army, broke their word to God (to let the Jews leave).

309   **sojourners of Goshen**   the Jews, who journeyed to Goshen on the far side of the Nile.

313   **amazement**   shock, bewilderment; also suggests wandering in a maze.

315   **Princes, potentates**   as usual, Satan begins his speech with a flattering *exordium* or address; see the outline of speech construction at the beginning of the Notes to Book 2. What emotions does Satan appeal to in this speech?

319–20   **to repose/Your wearied virtue**   one of several sarcastic taunts (continuing until 325); do you think it would be better or worse if Satan apologized for the defeat?

322–3   **abject, adore**   the assonance on *a* links the two words, suggesting one has to be thrown down (*abject*) to worship. See Interpretations page 159 on assonance.

324   **Cherub and seraph**   angelic beings.

325   **arms and ensigns**   weapons and flags.

      anon   soon. Satan is alerting them to immediate danger.

326–7   **discern/Th'advantage**   see that we are at their mercy.

328   **linkèd thunderbolts**   by taking the 'bolts' literally, Milton suggests chains made of thunder.

330   **Awake, arise**   note the arousing rhythm of this line.

The fallen angels rally and assemble before Satan: Lines 331–75

The angels seem to feel guilty (*abashed, found by whom they dread*); is this appropriate? The epic similes (see Interpretations pages 152–3) which describe them concentrate on their immense numbers, and yet comparisons with *locusts* and barbarian hordes from the *frozen loins* of the North diminish our respect for them. Milton then introduces the next substantial section of the poem, by explaining he will call the fallen angels by the *new names* of the pagan gods which they supposedly later became according to one tradition; can Milton possibly believe this to be literally true?

335–6   There are two double negatives here which cancel each other out (see Interpretations page 155), so that the angels do *perceive their plight* and *feel* their *pains*.

338–44   An epic simile comparing the fallen angels to the plague of locusts which Moses (*Amram's son*) called up by his supernaturally powerful (*potent*) rod to help persuade the *impious Pharaoh* to let the Jews go (Exodus 6:20, 10:12–15). Can you think of other points of comparison, besides their being *numberless*, between the fallen angels and a mass of insects which darken the sky, and then eat all the crops?

340   **pitchy**   black.

341   **warping**   whirling through the air like snow.

342   **impious**   irreligious (both because Pharaoh is a pagan, and because he breaks his oath to the Jews and their God).

345   **cope**   canopy.

346 **nether**   lower.

348 **sultan**   despot.

349 **in even balance down they light**   they alight in an ordered formation (at a signal from Satan's spear).

351–5 An epic simile comparing the angels to the *multitude* of barbarian invaders whom Machiavelli had described coming from the lands north of the Rhine and Danube (*Rhene or the Danaw*) to overturn the Roman Empire as far south as North Africa (*the Libyan sands*).

352 **frozen loins**   cold womb; perhaps rather extreme language for North Germany, but it is the first of a series of images suggesting 'false creativity' or sterility; see Interpretations page 168.

357 **The heads and leaders thither haste**   the leaders of each division of Satan's army advance quickly to be reviewed.

359 **princely dignities**   of royal status.

360 **erst**   before.

361–3 **their names... from the Books of Life**   the names they had in Heaven, such as Lucifer (which was Satan's), have been deleted from God's book of the blessed (see Revelation 21:27 and Interpretations page 177).

364 **sons of Eve**   derogatory term for humankind (because Eve was faithless).

365 **new names**   see headnote.

366 **God's high sufferance for the trial of Man**   God's allowance of liberty to the fallen angels so they can test humankind; see 1:213.

369–70 **th'invisible... to transform**   the fallen angels, by telling lies (*falsities*, 367) persuade men to worship them in the form of idols decorated with tinsel (*gay religions*, 372), instead of the invisible true God. Milton, as a Protestant, may be thinking of the Catholics as well as pagans here; see pages 7–8.

The parade of angels as pagan gods: Lines 376–521

A new invocation *Say Muse* (see note to 1:6) alerts us to a new episode, and a catalogue of heroes typical of classical epic (see Interpretations page 150). As explained in the previous headnote, Milton is using an old tradition that *long after* the fall of the angels from Heaven, they were worshipped on Earth as the pagan gods. Satan's commanders are a select group of these: the pagan gods chosen for worship by the Jewish kings themselves, who had temples near or even on Mount Sion, where the Temple to Jehovah stood (I Kings 11:7–9; II Kings 18:10–18; 21:1–5). The implication is that if even God's chosen people, the Jews, chose to follow pagan gods and the vices they represent, then Christians nowadays might also be tempted to follow the 'gods' of violence, self-indulgence, materialism, and so forth. Satan's commanders are, therefore, the representatives not of heroic but of degraded human qualities (see Interpretations page 177). As you read, keep thinking of the modern equivalents.

The whole passage (like its parallel in his *Nativity Ode* 197–228) exhibits Milton's knowledge of Hebrew and Jewish scholarship, but maybe the place names are chosen as much for their music as their authenticity (see Interpretations pages 159–60). As it is is very long, it is divided here into sub-sections (a–f) after a brief introductory section.

377	**fiery couch**	the burning lake.
379	**Came singly**	each named leader comes before Satan in the parade in order of importance (*worth*, 378).
	strand	beach.
380	**promiscuous**	undiscriminated.
382	**prey**	human beings to tempt and corrupt.
385	**durst abide**	dared endure (by being so close).
386–7	**throned/Between the cherubim**	there were gold cherubim at each end of the sacred Ark of the Covenant in the Temple which was on Mount *Sion* (Psalm 80:1).
388	**Within his sanctuary**	altars to pagan gods were set up within the Temple itself (see II Kings 21:1–5).
389	**Abominations**	pagan gods (the word used in the Authorized Version quoted in the next headnote).
391	**affront**	insult.

a) Moloch and Chemos: Lines 392–418

Milton puts at the front the gods whose temples were the greatest *affront* (391) to *Jehovah*, the true God. In I Kings 11:7–9 Solomon (under his wives' influence, of course) built 'a high place for Chemos, the abomination of Moab, in the hill that is before Jerusalem, and for Moloch, the abomination of the children of Ammon. And likewise did he for all his foreign wives, who burned incense and sacrificed unto their gods. And the Lord was angry with Solomon.' What vices do these two gods suggest to you?

392   **Moloch**   see Interpretations page 177. Moloch will be the first speaker in the debate in Book 2 (see line 51). Milton follows the historian Sandys in describing him as an idol with a furnace in his chest in which children were burned as sacrifices while priests drowned their cries 'with the continual clang of trumpets and timbrels' (tambourines). (See *A Relation of a Journey* (1637), Fowler edition of *P.L.*)

    horrid king   horrific king (*Moloch* means *king*).

396   **Ammonite**   followers of Moloch living in *Rabba*, the 'city of waters' (II Samuel 12:27) and in *Argob* and *Basan*, which were also in Judah (Judges 11:13).

400   **Audacious neighbourhood**   presumptuous position (in Judah).

403   **opprobrious hill**   (*hill of scandal* at 416) the shameful idol-covered hill 'before Jerusalem' (see headnote a), later the Mount of Olives, *against* (opposite) Jehovah's Temple on Mount Sion.

404–5   The valley that divided these hills was therefore discredited, lost the name *Hinnon*, and acquired the shameful names *Tophet* and *Gehenna* which were associated with Hell.

406   **Chemos**   the Moabite god; see headnote a) and Numbers 21:29.

407–11   These biblical place names, like *Sittim* (413) were associated with the Moabites.

411   **th'asphaltic pool**   the Dead Sea, which contains bitumens (inflammable minerals), such as asphalt.

412   **Peor**   Baal-Peor was another name for Chemos, whom the Jews briefly worshipped during their escape from Egypt.

414–15   **wanton rites, lustful orgies**   sexual licence associated with Chemos/Peor.

414   **cost them woe**   the Jews who worshipped Peor were punished by a plague (*woe*); see Numbers 25:1–9.

416   **hill of scandal**   see Note to 1:403.

417   **lust hard by hate**   the two temples, to Moloch and to Chemos, like these vices they represent, were very close to (*hard by*) each other.

418   **Josiah**   the king who destroyed the two temples and turned the valley to a rubbish dump (II Kings 23:13).

b) Baalim, Ashtaroth, and Thammuz: Lines 419–56

Milton now considers the sun-gods *Baalim* (plural of the generalized name Baal, 'Lord'), and the moon-goddess *Ashtareth* (plural *Ashtoreth*) who loved the beautiful youth *Thammuz*. They were worshipped in the area stretching from Canaan up as far as the Euphrates, and the cult of Thammuz in particular was associated with excessive emotionalism. Is Milton raising the question of which vices are 'gender-specific'? But if so, why is he so insistent that neither evil nor good spirits have any particular name, number, gender or shape (421–31)? Where in Books 1 and 2 do we see the angels change shape or size, becoming *Dilated or condensed*? See Interpretations page 154 for a discussion.

420	**brook**	the river Besor (I Samuel 30:10).
423	**spirits**	good as well as bad angels.
425	**essence**	the *quintessence* (3:716) or *empyreal substance* (1:117) from which the angels are made. As Raphael explains in more detail in 8:620–9 it is so pure (*uncompounded*) that angels can flow into one another when making love.
426	**manacled**	as Man (note the pun), unlike the angels, is a mixture of soul and body, his hands (*mains*) and other limbs act as handcuffs (*manacles*) chaining the free spirit inside the body.
427	**founded on the brittle strength**	based on fragile physical strength (as opposed to the *living strength* of God (433; see I Samuel 15:29).
431	**love or enmity**	depending on whether they are good or evil spirits).
432–7	**For those**	for Baal and Ashtaroth (see Judges 2:13–14 where the Jews 'forsook the Lord, and served Baal and Ashtaroth... And the Lord... delivered them into the hands of spoilers... and enemies').
435	**bestial**	beast-like in form or nature (as *brutish* at 1:481).
438–9	**Astoreth... Astartè**	the moon, here a horned goddess, is often associated with women (who have a monthly cycle). Phoenecia is on the coast of Syria and contains the city of Sidon (hence *Sidonian*).
442–3	**Sion... offensive mountain**	see Note to 403 above.
444	**uxorious**	over-fond of his (700) wives (see headnote a).
446	**Thammuz**	the youth known in Greece as *Adonis*, whom *Astarte* loved and revived from death; this was celebrated annually as part

of a fertility cult in Lebanon in late summer, when the Adonis river runs red with earth, suggesting his blood running from the boar-wound which had killed him (*yearly wounded*, 452).

453   The Jewish women (*Sion's daughters*) also began to express sorrow (*like heat*) for Thammuz, and this led to sexual rites which Ezekiel saw in a vision (Ezekiel 8:14). What is the connection which Milton seems to be making between sorrow and sex here?

457   **alienated Judah**   the Jews in exile in Babylon.

c) Dagon and Rimmon: Lines 457–76

The Philistines of Palestine (which contained the cities *Azotus, Gath, Ascalon, Accaron,* and *Gaza*) captured the holy Ark of the Jews, their traditional enemies, and put it in the temple of Dagon. The next morning the idol had lost its human head and hands; only its fish-tail was left (I Samuel 5:1–5). Rimmon was a Damascan god whom the Jewish king Ahaz worshipped (so that he *gained a king,* 471).

459   **Maimed**   see headnote c).

460   **grunsel**   threshold.

467   **Him followed Rimmon**   Rimmon came after Dagon (who presumably jumps along on his tail).

467–71   Rimmon's temple (*delightful seat*) was in Damascus on the confluence of the rivers *Abbana* and *Pharphar*, in which the *leper* Naaman said he would prefer to bathe, after Elisha told him to bathe in the Jordan – which he eventually did and was cured (II Kings 5:1–19) and so *lost* to Rimmon's worship.

472   **Ahaz his sottish conqueror**   the foolish Ahaz who displaced one of Jehovah's altars in the Temple by a copy of Rimmon's altar, although he had *vanquished* (476) Damascas and so should have appreciated the superiority of Jehovah (see II Kings 16:10–15).

d) The Egyptian gods: Lines 476–89

Milton identifies the Golden Calf worshipped by the Jews in *Oreb* (Exodus 32:1–6) with the *brutish* bovine gods of Egypt, from where they were escaping. Thus, like the Canaanite gods he has mentioned, these too represent a false choice made by the 'people of God' in the Bible. Since humankind is distinguished from beasts by possessing a soul and reason, to choose to worship a beast is to deliberately degenerate. What modern equivalent can you think of for such a false choice?

478   **Osiris, Isis, Orus**   *Osiris* was worshipped as a bull, *Isis* had cow's horns, and *Orus* was their calf-child.

479–80   **abused/Fanatic Egypt**   deceived the extremist priests of Egypt. The fallen angels took animal shapes (*monstrous*, *brutish*) or heads, and induced the Egyptians to worship them.

481   **wandering gods**   Isis wandered the world seeking the parts of Osiris' body.

      brutish forms   see headnote d) and Note to 1:435.

483   **Th'infection**   see line 453 above.

      borrowed   the priest Aaron took the golden earrings of the Jews to make the Golden Calf; see headnote d).

484   **rebel king**   Jeroboam, who later set up two (*Doubled*) golden calves, in *Bethel* and *Dan* in Sumaria (I Kings 12:20–29). These, like the original Golden Calf, were said to have delivered the Jews from Egypt (Psalm 106:20).

487–9   On the 'Passover' night God *passed* over the Jewish houses, but made the Egyptian first-born as dead (*equalled*) as their own gods; this *stroke* was the real reason for the Jews' deliverance from Egypt (Exodus 12:29–33).

489   **bleating**   cry of calves as well as sheep.

e) Belial: Lines 490–505

Belial has no altar because he was not really a distinct god in the Bible; the phrase *the sons/Of Belial* (501–2) seems to represent people enslaved to a group of vices rather than a specific idol. Using the biblical references Milton invents a new character, and gives him the vices of the rich in *courts and palaces*: atheism, gluttony, luxury, lust, violence, drunkenness, and sodomy. He is the second speaker in the debate in Book 2. Are these the vices he displays in 2:119–228? See Interpretations page 177. What does the phrase *to love/Vice for itself* (491–2) suggest to you?

490   **last**   of the named gods/angels.

491   **gross**   blatant.

495   **Eli's sons**   sons of the priest who preferred to eat rather than to sacrifice holy animals (I Samuel 2:12–17), suggesting the vice of greed.

500	**injury and outrage** insults and violation of others' rights.
	night as usual (for example, 1:440 above) Milton associates vice with darkness; see Interpretations page 166.
502	**flown** 'high flown' or 'high' in the modern sense.
503–5	In both *Sodom* and *Gibeah* a woman is offered to the *sons of Belial* by a *hospitable* Jew wishing to protect male guests from homosexual (*worse*) rape (Genesis 19:4–11; Judges 19: 22–28).

f) The classical gods: Lines 506–21

Having named the biblical gods, Milton describes the classical gods much more briefly, because the Jews never followed them. Why also might he not not want to associate them with vice or betrayal?

508	**Ionian gods** the Olympian gods.
	Javan a descendant of Noah and the supposed ancestor of the Greek race (Genesis 10:2).
	held believed.
509–10	They admitted themselves that they were younger than Uranus (*Heaven*) and Ge (*Earth*), whom they proudly claimed as their great-grandparents (their parents were the Titans).
512	**Saturn** the youngest of the Titans, said here to be the children (*brood*) of Uranus's eldest son, *Titan*. Saturn deposed his father and was himself deposed in the same way (*like measure*) by Zeus (*Jove*), the son he had by *Rhea*. These *usurping* acts repeat the sin of Satan; see Note to 1:197–200 and Interpretations page 149.
514–15	**Crete/And Ida** Mount Ida in Crete was believed to be the birthplace of Zeus (and tourists are even shown his bath).
516	**Olympus** the gods supposedly inhabited the highest mountain in Greece, Olympus, which is always snow-covered.
516–17	**middle air... heaven** the air at the level of mountain tops which is the part inhabited by spirits who cannot reach the *empyrean* (God's Heaven).
517–18	**Delphi, Dodona** places in Greece (*Doric land*) where the classical gods were *renowned* (507) for oracles. Note the dreamy effect of the alliteration.
519	**or who** further examples of *The rest* (507), this time from outside Greece.
519–21	**with Saturn... utmost isles** after being deposed, Saturn fled over the Adriatic Sea (*Adria*) through Italy (*th'Hesperian fields*) and France (*Celtic*) to Britain (*utmost isles*) where he may still lie asleep on Anglesey.

Satan comforts and marshals the fallen angels: Lines 522–87

Satan seems here to show genuine concern for his army, and he encourages them by calling them to arms, though as usual there are words which might undermine this positive impression. Should we be impressed by him? Should we feel an increasing admiration for the angels? They do seem to be trying to recover from their *abject posture* on the burning lake, when their arms lay *scattered* around them (see 1:322, 325). There are a number of upward-moving (for example *upreared, upsent*) and brightening (*meteor, lustre*) words associated with them, but perhaps this recovery should be seen as superficial and temporary. Why does Milton compare them to armies which seem more fictional than real – first the classical soldiers dancing to *Dorian* music, and then the armies of Italian epics and English and French romances (see Interpretations page 150)? Should we be thinking of the heroic qualities and vast spectacle of such armies, or of their unreality?

523	**such wherein** such *looks* (522) in which.
525	**despair** see Note to 1:126.
527	**Like doubtful hue** the same ambiguous expression.
527–8	**wonted pride/Soon recollecting** quickly summoning up his usual pride.
529	**Semblance... not substance** the appearance of value, not the reality.
529–30	What do *gently* and *dispelled* tell you about Satan? Why does Milton feel he must interpose his own voice to discredit Satan's words as having *Semblance of worth, not substance* (they only seemed valuable and true)?
531	**straight** immediately.
532	**clarions** shrill military trumpets.
533–6	**standard, imperial ensign** Satan's personal flag.
534	**Azazel** one of Satan's four standard bearers according to Jewish 'cabbalistic' (occult) writings, in which Milton was keenly interested.
537–9	The flag was decorated (*emblazed*) like a Roman standard with jewels, shining gold thread, coats of arms, and battle souvenirs. What does the comparison to a *meteor* suggest to you (see Note to 1:594–9 for one suggestion)?

540	**Sonorous metal** the resonant instruments mentioned in 532 above.
541	**the universal host upsent** the whole army sent up (the last word is turned round to fit the metre; see Interpretations page 158).
542	**tore Hell's concave** penetrated the arched roof (see 1:298).
543	**reign of Chaos** the kingdom outside Hell, ruled by *Chaos* and his consort, *Night* (we meet them in 2:959–63; see Interpretations pages 180–1).
546	**orient** lustrous, bright.
547	**helms** helmets.
548	**serried** close-packed.
549	**depth immeasurable** it was impossible to measure the width of the column. (One of several places where Milton suggests that the fallen angels are numberless; see page 11).
550	In exact formation to appropriate modal music. The Dorian mode (*mood*), which is the white-note scale beginning on D, was associated in ancient Greece with military music.
551–9	Milton, an ardent musician (see Interpretations page 156), here describes the effect of music, as he does again in 2:546–55; in both cases emotions are controlled and soothed (*swage*) rather than aroused. The Dorian music here also seems able to control virtue, by transforming the emotion of rage into a steely composure (*noblest temper*) and willed courage (*Deliberate valour*). Aristotle said that this mode induced a 'settled temper' and Plato said it gave courage. (Prince ed. of *P.L.*)
556–7	**Nor wanting… thoughts** not lacking power to lessen and soothe *troubled thoughts* by brief serious phrases (*solemn touches*).
558	Note the soothing effect of the repeated *and*.
560–1	**Breathing united force… in silence** compare Homer's *Iliad* 3:8: 'The Greeks marched in silence, breathing courage.'
561	**charmed** are the angels being deluded by the music?
563	**horrid front** the front line bristling with spears (see Note to 1:51).
568	**traverse** across.
570	**visages and stature** faces and size.
571	**number** see Note to 549 above.
572	**Distends… and hardening** enlarges, puffs up, and then hardens (compare Daniel 5:20 where God deposes King Nebuchadnezzar because 'his heart was lifted up, and his mind hardened in pride'). But do you altogether despise Satan here?

573–6   **for never… cranes**   for never since the creation of humankind could a concentrated (*embodied*) human force be assembled which, when compared to these, would be worth more than the Pygmy army. Pygmies are a race of very small people in Africa who (according to *Iliad* III 1–5) were frequently attacked and defeated by flocks of cranes (birds); they are referred to again in 1:780.

575   **infantry**   foot-soldiers (with a pun on infant, suggesting smallness).

576   **though**   even if; introduces a comparison of Satan's army with the lesser ones of the Greek, Arthurian, and French legends.

576–8   **giant brood… Ilium**   even if the Titans (already mentioned in 198 and 510) who fought the Olympian gods at *Phlegra* were joined with the gods and Greek heroes who fought at *Thebes* and Troy (*Ilium*).

579   **auxiliar**   helping (according to Homer, the Greek gods were involved in these human wars).
         resounds   is famous.

580   **romance of Uther's son**   stories (known collectively as *romances*) of King Arthur, son of Uther Pendragon, and his surrounding (*Begirt*) Round Table of knights from Britain and Brittany (*Armorica*).

581   **Begirt**   surrounded.

582–7   Milton finally refers to the legendary armies of the ninth-century Emperor Charlemagne (*Charlemain*), who defended France from Muslim (*infidel*) and African invaders until he and his 12 chief knights (*peerage*) were defeated at Roncesvalles (not *Fontarabbia*). The hypnotic place-names are mostly from Italian epics like *Orlando Furioso* (see Interpretations page 150).

583   **Jousted**   fought on horseback with lances.

585   **Biserta**   the port from which the African king Agramante embarked.

Third description of Satan: He weeps for his army: Lines 587–621

Here we are told of the physical and moral degeneration of Satan, but we may feel how much remains (including what remains of his virtue) rather than how much is lost. The comparisons of Satan with a tower and the obscured sun suggest he is god-like, as these are similes for

God in the Bible (for example, II Samuel 22:3; Psalms 84:11), but also note words which suggest he is damaged and dangerous (for example, *ruined*). He seems very human here, and we are allowed to share in his feelings, although he seems determined to conceal them even from himself. Look at words like *followers* and *faithful*, used of the army. Does Satan's *remorse* make his continuing the war more or less forgivable?

587–8	**Thus far... yet observed**	although these were so far above comparison, yet Satan could see them all.
594–9	**as when... monarchs**	epic similes comparing Satan to the sun obscured by mist or the shadow of the moon. Since God is more naturally associated with the sun, and Satan with the moon (see Interpretations page 154), what does the *misty air* and *dim eclipse* which change the sun's light here suggest about Satan?
595	**horizontal**	a transferred epithet as it is the *beams*, not the *air*, which are *horizontal*. Note the assonance with *Shorn* in 596.
597–9	**disastrous twilight... monarchs**	eclipses, like comets, were supposed to predict natural disasters and political unrest, particularly as one accompanied Christ's death (Luke 23:44); in what ways will Satan have this effect?
601	**thunder**	the weapon which cast him out of Heaven (see Note to 1:93).
	entrenched	furrowed.
603	**dauntless**	fearless.
	considerate	deliberate (from Latin *considerare*, meaning to think).
606	**fellows... followers**	one letter shifts the meaning from companion to victim.
607	Compare with 1:84.	
609–10	**amerced/Of Heaven**	fined or deprived of Heaven.
612–15	**As when... blasted heath**	epic simile comparing the army to a lightning-struck forest left standing on burnt soil (*blasted heath*); compare 1:292–6 above. What does the phrase *stately growth* (referring to branches) tell you about the angels?
616–18	The main body of the army forms a close semi-circle around Satan and the other leaders (*peers*).	
619	**essayed**	tried (to speak).
	scorn	his own pride. Do you admire his tears or his suppression of them more?
621	**interwove**	interwoven, mixed.

Satan gives his army an account of the past and a plan for the future: Lines 622–69

This is Satan's first political speech and its purpose is to influence rather than inform his army, though he does tell them for the first time about Earth. What does he want them to feel, or not to feel? How does he characterize God? Do you think the complexity of the sentences suggests that Satan is hiding something?

Using the Latin terms listed at the beginning of the Notes to Book 2, we can divide the speech into the following sections:
• the flattering address or **exordium** (622–3)
• the first argument or **narratio** (626–30) which attempts to explain the past, and is supported by three **confirmationes** or supporting arguments (631–4, 635–7, 637–42)
• the second **narratio** (643–56), which looks to the future, and is supported by one confirmatio (657–9)
• the **conclusio** summoning a council (659–62) and giving the motion for debate (what kind of war to pursue).

622	**myriads**	vast numbers (see page 11).
624	**not inglorious... dire**	glorious even if the outcome was terrible.
625	**testifies**	witnesses, proves.
626–31		Satan's first argument (the narratio and confirmatio of 626–42) is that no-one, however prophetic or knowledgeable, could have *feared* (main verb) failure. Note how the rhetorical questions and the repeated auxiliaries (*could... could... can*) communicate his incredulity.
627	**presaging**	predicting.
630	**repulse**	check.
631–4		For no-one could believe they will fail to *re-ascend*, even though they are now (*yet*) experiencing loss. The argument that the angels, being made of fire, the lightest element, will re-ascend, is used again at 2:75–6.
632	**puissant legions**	powerful divisions.
633	**emptied Heaven**	in fact (5:710) only a third of the angels were cast out.

634   **native seat**   original homeland (implying they have a right to be there).

635–7   **be witness... our hopes**   I call all angels to vouch for the truth that it was not because I took the wrong advice, or tried to avoid dangers, that we lost. Does this absolve him of responsibility for the failure?

639–40   **old repute,/Consent or custom**   three reasons for retaining the monarchy: its fame, its acceptance by the people, and its long history. Sneering at these means Satan has to find other reasons for justifying his own rule at 2:18–21. For Milton's own contempt for monarchy, see page 3.

640   **regal state**   royal grandeur (as opposed to practical *strength*, 641).

642   **tempted our attempt**   the pun reinforces the lie that God enticed them to attack him by appearing weak.

        wrought   made, brought about.

643–56   Satan's second narratio. God creates the universe after the fall of the angels (see page 12), but Satan says he has heard a rumour of the plan, though he prefers to see *Space* as the creative force; we hear more about his plan at 2:380.

644–5   **So as not... provoked**   we will neither provoke nor respond if God provokes us (again note the characterization of God).

646–7   **To work... effected not**   to plan secretly (*close design*) how *fraud or guile* may achieve what *force* failed to achieve.

648–9   **who overcomes... foe**   the whole phrase is the object of *find*.

650   **rife**   prevalent.

651   **ere long**   before long (see Note to 643–56).

653–4   Both here and at the next mention of humankind (2:345–51) we feel Satan inflaming the jealousy of the other angels (*sons of Heaven*).

656   **eruption**   ascent (but it sounds distorted and violent).

660   **Peace is despaired**   we have abandoned hope of peace (though this is not true of the angels: see 2:227, 292).

662   **understood**   one of a number of words in the speech to suggest a policy of a secret, deceitful hostility.

663   **out-flew**   flew out (like *upsent*, 541 above).

666   **illumined**   lit up (see Interpretations page 168).

666–7   **highly... Highest**   what is the effect of the pun?

668   **Clashed**   a traditional Roman 'hurrah' was to clash swords on shields.

The building of Pandæmonium: Lines 670–751

Pandæmonium is Milton's invented name for the infernal Parliament building. It is built on the model of a Greek temple, appropriate for the classical soldiers which the angels are impersonating at the moment. It also has the ornateness which Milton may have seen in Italy in classical-style Catholic churches such as St Peter's cathedral in Rome. Its aesthetic values are those of Heaven (see Revelation 21, the illustration on page 8, and pages 168–9), but its imagery is that of a rather gross human body (*Belched, scurf, womb*, etc.; see Interpretations page 161). Is it a noble attempt to make *a Heaven of Hell* (1:255) or merely an imitation, a theatrical, temporary, empty illusion?

670	**grisly**	horrifying.
674	**The work of sulphur**	sulphur (characterized by a flaky *scurf*) was supposed to be the agent which produced the other metals.
675–8	**As when... a rampart**	epic simile comparing the angels to foot-soldiers (*pioneers*) preparing a battlefield; what is the effect of the comparison?
677	**Forerun**	go before an army to make preparations.
678	**cast**	throw up.
	Mammon	the biblical personification of wealth and worldly values; see Matthew 6:24, Luke 16:13 and Interpretations page 178.
679	**least erected**	most ignoble (he speaks last at the Council).
681	**downward bent**	directions are crucial in Milton (see pages 13–15), for love, virtue, and creativity should always be directed towards God and not away from him or into the self.
682	**Heaven's pavement**	in Revelation 21:21 we are told that 'the street of the [heavenly] city was pure gold, as it were transparent glass'.
683–4	**aught divine... vision beätific**	anything else which the angelic and mystical (*beatific*) vision was able to enjoy.
685	**Men also**	the classical author Ovid saw the mining of wealth from Mother Earth as part of the fall of Man from the original Golden Age (*Metamorphosis* I 137–42), and Spenser has Mammon mining gold in Hell in *Faerie Queene* II 7 (1596; see Interpretations page 150).

686	**impious** irreligious, disrespectful.
687–90	**bowels, wound, ribs,** more body imagery (see Interpretations page 161 for the suggestion of rape).
690	**admire** wonder at.
692	**precious bane** valuable poison (an oxymoron; see Interpretations page 167).
694	**Babel** the tower of Babel aimed to 'reach unto Heaven' (Genesis 11:4–9).
	Memphian kings the Egyptian kings or pharaohs built the enormous pyramids near Cairo (*Memphis*); compare 2:483–5.
697	**reprobate** rejected, proved bad.
	in an hour note here and at 711 the speed with which the edifice is built; what does this suggest to you?
700	**Nigh** nearby.
	cells workshops (with underfloor furnaces).
702	**Sluiced** channelled.
703	**founded** (*found out* in the second edition) melted (main verb) as in a foundry.
703–4	By their *art* or skill they separate the ores and skim the impurities (*dross*) from the pure metals (*bullion*). Or maybe *bullion dross* is another oxymoron?
705	**A third** a third group (the first mined, the second smelted).
706–7	A complex mould (representing the shape of the whole building carved in reverse into the ground) into whose detailed indentations the molten metal is conveyed, by a clever system, forming a hollow shape.
708–12	Just as one expulsion of wind (*blast, exhalation*) can fill many *organ* pipes, so a musical breath filled the mould from underneath and blew the hollow building inside-out on top of the ground (like a plastic toy). What is suggested to you by this pneumatic building method and sound effects (712)?
710	**Anon** at once.
711	**exhalation** outburst of air or wind (suggesting what?).
712	**dulcet symphonies** sweet instrumental music. Musical proportions were supposedly allied to architectural ones, so Thebes and Troy were also constructed to the sound of music.
713–14	**pilasters round/Were** squared columns were arranged around (probably against the wall).
714–16	**Doric pillars... graven** an inner colonnade of *pillars* with *Doric* capitals (same connotations as the music at 1:550) supported the

golden beam (*architrave*) leading up to a projecting *Cornice*, on
which was carved in high relief (*bossy sculptures*) the decorative
frieze. The architrave could go across the front or around the
whole space. The effect is classically impressive but clearly
pagan.

717   **fretted**   carved in decorative patterns usually of intersecting
lines; Hamlet admired the heavens 'fretted with golden fire'
(II 2.313). Though the angels themselves have never seen the sky,
we recognize their roof is an imitation.

717–18   **Babylon, Alcairo**   monumental capital cities of the oppressive
kingdoms of Assyria and Egypt; Babylon was in particular the
focus of evil in the Bible (Revelation 17:5) and became an
insulting name for Rome, home of the Pope. See the gigantic
Assyrian sculptures in the British Museum.

720   **Belus, Serapis**   the Assyrian form of Baal, and the Egyptian
Osiris; see Note to 419–56 and 478 above.

722–3   **Th'ascending pile/Stood fixed**   the edifice stopped rising at its
proper height. In 1637 a court masque (musical entertainment)
included a scene where 'the earth open'd, and there rose up a
richly-adorned pallace... with proticos vaulted, on pillasters of rich
rustick work; their bases and capitels of gold. Above these ran an
architrave, freese, and coronis of the same' (quoted from
M. Hughes ed. of *P.L*). In what ways is Pandæmonium like a piece
of theatrical scenery?

724   **brazen folds**   brass leaves.
      discover   reveal (but what do they reveal? Compare 2:890).

727   **subtle magic**   clever contrivance (as opposed to God's ability to
hang the stars in the sky).

728–9   **lamps... naphtha and asphaltus**   lamps containing oil from
bituminous rock (*naphtha*) and hanging baskets (*cressets*) holding
lumps of burning asphalt; the ingredients of Hell used to
imitate the heavenly city which 'had no need of the sun,
neither of the moon... for the glory of God did lighten it'
(Revelation 21:23).

734   **sceptred angels**   high-ranking angels who lived in towers.

736   **Exalted**   glorified.

737   **hierarchy**   his place in the hierarchy of *orders*, as in an army (see
page 12). How do you respond to this glimpse of heavenly society?
Does it suggest the monarchy and perhaps nobility which Milton
himself had sought to overthrow (see page 3)? Or does it symbolize
creation's ordered ascent to God (see pages 13–14)?

739–40   **in Ausonian land… Mulciber**   in Italy (*Ausonia*) men
called the Greek god Hephaestus *Mulciber* (or Vulcan). As smith
and artist he built the palaces of the gods on Mount Olympus
before he was thrown down by Zeus (*Iliad* I 588–95).

746   **Lemnos th'Ægæan isle**   *Lemnos* in the Ægæan sea, where
Mulciber landed.

747   **Erring**   Milton claims that the story of the fall of Mulciber
is a misrepresentation of the true story of the fall of the angels
(1:44–9 above; see page 12 and Isaiah 14:12–15). Why does Milton
make Mulciber sound so beautiful, and why does he emphasize
this word by its position?

748   **nor aught availed**   nor did it help him.

750   **engines**   contrivances (such as the *subtle magic* of 727).

The fallen angels take possession of Pandæmonium: Lines 752–98

Having done so much to magnify and glorify the angels, Milton seems
here to be using mock-epic techniques to diminish them in our eyes.
A mock epic laughs at the form and the heroic qualities of the epic
(discussed in Interpretations page 151); Pope's *Rape of the Lock* is an
example. The passage is almost a comic interlude before the solemn
business of Book 2. What do the comparisons with insects (compare
1:341), Pygmies, and elves suggest to you? Why does Milton have
them change both their costume and their size?

753   **sovereign power**   Satan's royal power.
      awful   awe-inspiring.

756   **Pandæmonium**   'All the Demons' (Milton's coinage from Greek
words, which has come to mean a chaotic assembly).

758   **squarèd**   drawn up in a square.

759   **By place or choice the worthiest**   representatives to attend the
Parliament are chosen by rank or election. Should we compare this
democracy to the rigid hierarchy of Heaven (see 1:737)?

763–6   Milton compares the hall to a huge crowded tent where
Saracen knights were challenged (*Defied*) before their sultan's
(*soldan's*) throne. Saracens were the Muslim (*paynim*)
opponents of the Christians in the Crusades; this continues

the Romance comparisons of 579–87 above; the angels seem to have now changed their costume from that of the classical army.

766 **career with lance** jousting, or horseback fighting with lances.

768 Note the onomatopoeic alliteration (see Interpretations page 159).

768–75 Epic simile comparing the angels to bees active in spring-time (when the sun enters *Taurus* in April). Some swarm *In clusters*, others collect nectar from flowers; others walk about and discuss (*expatiate and confer*) on the *plank* that goes into the hive, which is *rubbed* with attractive oils (*balm*). Of course they only imagine they have control over *Their state affairs*. How many more points of comparison can you find between the bees and the angels, and what is the effect on your attitude to them?

773 **straw-built citadel** castle built of straw (compare the *Three Little Pigs*).

776 **straitened** confined into too narrow a space.

777–80 The innumerable angels shrink themselves from the size of giants to tiny elves. See discussion in Interpretations page 154 and compare the visual effects at 1:284–95.

781 **Indian mount** the Himalayas, beyond which the classical historian Pliny erroneously located the pygmies, who really live in central Africa.

781–8 **or fairy elves... rebounds** epic simile comparing the diminished angels with elves. Note the care with which Milton sets the scene at night (as at 1:207), when the moon provokes and witnesses (*Sits arbitress*) magic and madness, and the fairies play sinister yet compelling music. How does the comparison warn us about the angels?

793–5 The chief angels (*seraphic lords*) have not diminished themselves, but sit in special seats in private council (*secret conclave*). What does this tell you about Satan's style of government?

797 **Frequent and full** crowded and without absentees.

798 **consult** consultation.

Notes to Book 2

The Argument to Book 2

Milton's outline of Book 2, like that of Book 1, focuses on Satan's role, and he does not name the other speakers at the *consultation*, nor the gatekeepers of Hell and the rulers of Chaos. The plan to subvert humankind is said to be *mentioned before by Satan*, and his courage and determination seem to be *honoured* by the author as well as his fellow angels.

6   **about this time**   see the Note to line 22 in the Argument to Book 1.
11   **who sat there**   i.e. Sin and Death.
12   **discover**   reveal.
13   **gulf**   Chaos the place, seen as both a hollow emptiness and full of the elements.
14   **Chaos**   Chaos the person, ruler of the kingdom of Chaos.

The Notes refer to the following sub-divisions of classical speeches (see Interpretations pages 162–5 on Milton's knowledge of these):

exordium   address often naming the people addressed (and note the effect of immediacy when this is not done).

narratio   statement of one argument (there can be more than one narratio).

confirmatio   evidence, proofs, arguments, and reasons for each narratio.

confutatio   refutation of objections, either imagined ones, or those raised by a previous speaker.

conclusio   a short recapitulation and proposal for action.

Modern and Renaissance rhetorical (speech-making) terms are explained in the section on Persuasion (Interpretations pages 162–3). In order to test the speeches against one another, ask the following questions about each:

Is the speaker's assessment of the situation
• true or mistaken
• a flattering delusion
• deliberately misleading?
Is his plan
• heroic or cowardly
• active or passive
• practical
• spiteful
• difficult or easy?

Satan's elevation and opening speech: Lines 1–42

Satan sits like a Pope or a king in Parliament. Note all the words suggesting height (*high*, *exalted*, *uplifted*); like Pandæmonium itself he is attempting to ascend towards Heaven. This speech, like his previous one (1:622–62), is notable for his self-justification and convoluted logic. Here he is explaining why he has remained their leader in spite of the disastrous failure of his last plan. He gives four reasons for his position (*just right*, *fixed laws*, the angels' *free choice*, his own *merit*) but fails to mention that it was God who gave him the responsibility of leadership in the first place. Do his claims have any grounds? The implicit parallel is with Jesus, who is genuinely elevated by merit (6:43, 758) and takes the greatest share of pain.

2–3   **Ormus... Ind... East**   Ormus (now Ormuz, an island town off the Persian coast), India, and the East generally were all famous for their jewels and the wealth and ostentation of their monarchs.

    4   'It was the eastern custom, at the coronation of their kings, to powder them with gold-dust and seed-pearl' (Warburton ed. of *P.L.*). **barbaric**   savage, pagan.

    6   **bad eminence**   an oxymoron; is he higher or essentially lower than the others?

6–9   These lines chart Satan's psychological progress in Book 1, though he cannot leave despair behind (see Interpretations pages 173–6).

    8   **Beyond thus high**   beyond this point. **insatiate**   ever hungry.

9   **success**   outcome (an earlier meaning); the irony of using it to mean 'failure' seems deliberate.

10   **imaginations**   fantasies.

11   This flattering exordium (see page 108) refers to two of the orders of angels; see page 12.

12–13   A theory expanded by Moloch in 2:75–81 that the *empyreal substance*, out of which the angels are made, naturally ascends and so must leave the depths (*gulf*) of Hell.

14–17   The idea that the fallen angels will have learned *Celestial virtues* from their fall, which will prevent a second fall, is a parody of Adam's 'fortunate fall' which taught him new virtues like humility and allowed the atonement of Christ (see page 13).

18–23   Satan argues that although he was already well-established as leader (giving the four reasons listed in the headnote), his failure has made him even more secure. Does this seem logical to you?

18   **just right**   something like the Divine Right with which Charles I vainly tried to protect his crown. For other claims, see headnote.

22   **recovered**   they are now *at least* better than they were at the beginning of Book 1.

23   **unenvied**   no-one could envy his throne now, so all grant him (*yield*) his position.

28   **the Thunderer's**   God's (see Note to 1:93).

29   **bulwark**   defensive rampart (he is a *tower* at 1:591).

32   **faction**   division or intrigue within a group. Milton may be remembering the problems in the armies during the Civil War (see page 4).

32–5   **for none... covet more**   Satan is claiming that the upside-down nature of Hell makes his *bad eminence* one of pain, not joy, but you might think that other angels *could* envy his position.

36   **faith... accord**   faithfulness and harmony. Milton praises their *concord* (2:496–7).

37–8   Can you find two lies here? (Claiming a *just inheritance* was a standard excuse for aggressive warfare.)

39–40   This chiasmus (a phrase in which words reappear in reversed order, see Interpretations page 164) conceals the illogicality of the argument, as *prosperity* generally does ensure one *prospers*.

41   **open war or covert guile**   the motion for the debate, which assumes that the decision to continue the war has already been made. In fact this decision is what the angels actually discuss; see Interpretations page 174.

Moloch's call to arms: Lines 43–105

Moloch was introduced as a *horrid king besmeared with blood* in 1:392–6 (see Interpretations page 177) who was both cruel and insensitive to others' pain. Though these attributes may be found in his speech, Milton says that like Satan, his thirst for revenge is grounded in *despair* because he recognizes God's genuine superiority, and his own misery in being deprived of the *bliss* of being near him. His speech is therefore essentially an appeal for mass suicide, though he presents it as a feasible plan. As befits a soldier, his style is plain, with few rhetorical figures, and no exordium, moving directly to his narratio in support of one of Satan's alternatives. It is worth distinguishing where he is truthful (for example, in his understanding of the difference between Hell and the Heaven they have lost), and where, like the other speakers, he 'packages' the truth (particularly about God).

43   **Moloch**   his name means king.

46   **deemed**   thought.

48–9   **with that care... fear**   because he cannot be what he cares about (equal with God), he fears nothing worse.

50   **recked**   cared.

51   **sentence**   judgement.

51–2   **of wiles... I boast not**   I do not offer suggestions for *covert guile* (41) as I am not an expert in this unmilitary field.

53   **Contrive who need**   let those who need to (who in fact include Satan) waste time in plotting rather than fighting. Note words which convey his urgency.

58   **opprobrious**   disgraceful, deserving reproach. Compare how other speakers refer to Hell, for example, 2:168, 254.

60–70   Moloch's narratio (see page 108).

62   **resistless**   impossible to resist.

63   **horrid arms**   terrible weapons.

65   **almighty engine**   the chariot pulled by cherubim described in Ezekiel 1:10 and used in *Paradise Lost* 6:749 by Jesus when he expels the rebel angels.

69   **Tartarean sulphur, and strange fire**   *Tartarus* was the part of Hades used for punishment. Hell's mineral composition was described in 1:670–4; the *Black fire* was mentioned in line 67 (and 1:62–3).

70   **His own invented torments**   as in 2:64 God is seen as a sadistic inventor of torture, but the fallen angels could be said to be their real inventors; see Interpretations page 167.

          But perhaps   first confutatio or refutation of a possible objection (see page 108).

73–4   **sleepy drench/Of that forgetful lake**   Moloch suggests contemptuously that having swallowed a drink (*drench*) from the lake of fire, the angels have become lethargic and forgetful, but we will learn that they are unable to reach the waters of Lethe which might have had that effect (2:604–14).

75   **proper motion**   natural movement (see Note to 1:631–4) as distinct from *adverse* (77).

78   The good angels followed Satan's rebels into Chaos (*the deep*); see 2:996–8.

82   **Th'event is feared**   Moloch's second confutatio, contradicting those who might fear the outcome (*event*) of another attack on God, which might make them *worse destroyed* (85). He answers with the rhetorical question *what can be worse?* (85), the phrase on which Belial builds his own confutatio of Moloch.

83   **Our Stronger**   a way of referring to God which itself indicates that they cannot win.

87   **abhorrèd deep**   suggests the distance from *bliss* (86) as well as Moloch's hatred of Hell.

89–92   **exercise, vassals, scourge, penance**   words which suggest that Hell is a place of punishment, either one where God makes them the slaves (*vassals*) to satisfy his *wrath* and sadism, or, perhaps more flatteringly, one where religious *exercises* like scourging are accepted as penance (Fowler ed. of *P.L.*).

93   **abolished and expire**   be annihilated and die. This suggestion that the *empyreal substance* is not in fact immortal is given a terrifying imaginative construction by Belial in 2:149–51 (see Interpretations page 164).

94–5   **what doubt… ire?**   why should we fear to provoke his most extreme anger?

97   **essential**   essence.

101   **On this side nothing**   as near as we can be to nothingness, and so unable to feel (is this an admirable desire?).

101–5   Moloch's 'conclusio' returns to his original suggestion for a mass assault on Heaven, though now he hopes only to *disturb* and *alarm* an *inaccessible* God.

104   **fatal**   fated to remain.

Belial's do-nothing policy: Lines 106–228

Belial is so persuasive that Milton warns us directly against believing him, both before (*But all was false*) and after his speech (*Counselled ignoble ease*). His appearance suggests a life of privilege (see his first appearance 1:490–505 and Interpretations page 177), encouraging the vices of selfishness and slothfulness as well as *lust and violence*. But he also seems more intelligent than Moloch in his 'confutationes' of each of Moloch's points, often quoting his words: *revenge, could we... rise, despair, woe*, etc. He also seems more cultivated in his use of rhetoric; though his language is often simple, he can evoke with terrifying or soothing effect the possible futures open to them (see for example the analysis of 142–59 in Interpretations pages 164–5). Is he persuasive? Does he or Moloch have the more realistic understanding of their situation?

109   **act**   manner.
        humane   polite.

113   **manna**   sweetness (sweets made from gum of the manna ash were supposed to evoke the heavenly food mentioned in Exodus 16 and Psalm 78).

113–14   **could make... better reason**   making the *worse* argument appear the *better* was associated with the logic-chopping Greek *Sophists*; the angels are compared to Greek philosophers again in 2:555–69.

114–15   **dash/Maturest counsels**   overthrow more considered advice.

116   **To vice industrious**   an oxymoron suggesting the reversed values of Hell, where Belial works hard to support vice.

119   Note the relaxed, almost chatty exordium (see page 108).

123   **Ominous conjecture**   possibility of things going wrong.
        success   outcome (see Note to 2:9).

124–7   **When he... dissolution**   when he who excels in warfare gives, as his *Main reason* (121) for pursuing an aggressive revenge-policy, the fact that they will at least escape the *utter* woe of Hell by annihilation.

126   **Mistrustful**   this prominently placed word undermines the two preceding *excels* to show Moloch's lack of faith in his own powers.

127   **scope**   extent.

130   **watch**   guards.
        render   make.

131   **Impregnable**   able to resist any attack.
        deep   Chaos, like the *realm of Night* (133).

132   **óbscure**   dark.

136   **insurrection, to confound**   uprising from Hell to defeat *Heaven's purest light* (137).

139   **th'ethereal mould**   airy form which angels were supposed to wear to make their immaterial bodies visible (see John Donne's *Air and Angels*: 'as an angel, face and wings/Of air, not pure as it, yet pure doth wear'); it also suggests the 'form' of God himself, which cannot be corrupted or polluted.

140–2   **Incapable... Victorious**   God, unable to be stained, would purge himself of the evil (*mischief*) and inferior (*baser*) fire of Hell by victory. (Note that Hell is feminized; see Interpretations page 162.)

142–6   **hope/Is flat despair... sad cure**   these paradoxes (that hope is utterly devoid of hope, that the cure brings sorrow, not healing) expose the self-contradictions in Moloch's argument.

149–50 Milton's Chaos includes all the materials for creation but is itself formless (*uncreated*); see 2:911. How do you respond to the two body-images here: *womb* and *swallowed*?

152   **Let this be good**   even if we allowed that annihilation is a good.

153   **it**   the annihilation described in 146–51, which might be incompatible with their *empyreal substance*, so that God cannot give it.

156   **Belike through impotence**   perhaps through lack of power (said sarcastically).

157–8   A chiasmus: the first phrase *end/Them in his anger* gives Moloch's expectation, which Belial then reverses (*whom his anger saves*) to give his own; see Interpretations page 164.

160   **Say they**   do they say? (introduces another confutatio).

160–3   Contemptuously echoes 85–7. *Decreed/Reserved and destined* are all words suggesting they are fated, a suggestion which the fallen angels usually prefer (see Interpretations page 176).

165   **amain**   at full speed.
        strook   struck.

166   **besought**   begged.

170   **the breath**   God's breath.

173   **intermitted vengeance**   interrupted (and so resumable) revenge. Satan observed in 1:169–77 that the angelic *ministers of vengeance* had returned to Heaven, and the *sulphurous hail* and *thunder* had stopped.

174	**red right hand** red with blood or fire; simple but terrifying words.

174 **red right hand**   red with blood or fire; simple but terrifying words.

175 **firmament**   sky, roof.

176–7 **cataracts... Impendent**   fiery waterfalls hanging over their heads.

179 **Designing or exhorting**   planning or urging (said sarcastically).

182 **racking**   torturing.

183 **yon**   yonder, over there (the lake of fire).

185 Without rest or pity or rescue. This line is scanned on page 159.

186 **Ages of hopeless end**   ages without hope of end.

187–8 Here Belial ceases his 'confutationes' and begins his 'narratio' on the motion.

190 In *De Doctrina* Milton repeats the ancient belief that God exists outside time, and so sees past, present, and future simultaneously (*at one view*); he is therefore impossible to surprise.

191 **motions**   proposals.
derides   scorns (echoing Psalm 2:4: 'the Lord shall have them in derision'); God does seem to do this, for example in 5:718.

192 **Not more**   just as.

196–7 **Better... advice**   my advice is that we should suffer these torments rather than risk worse.

197–8 **fate inevitable, omnipotent decree**   unchangeable fate, all-powerful command. In contradiction to his own argument at 160–1, Belial is stressing that God has no choice but to keep them in Hell. But as we learn from the forgiveness of Adam and Eve, God never restricts his options in this way. Belial, like Satan, is trying to limit the fallen angels' choices.

199 **To suffer, as to do**   as at 1:158, the choice before them is seen in terms of the classical division between acting and being acted upon (*suffering* in the archaic sense of *allowing*). Belial now has to 'package' the latter option, which Milton will call *sloth* (227), as noble endurance.

199–201 **To suffer... ordains**   it is just that if we are prepared to act, we should also be prepared to accept (*suffer*) the effects of action.

201–3 **this was at first... Contending**   if we think wisely, we will realize that the present suffering was an accepted possibility (*resolved*) from the first moment we decided to fight God.

205 **venturous**   daring
if that fail them   if the spear fails to give them victory.

207 **ignominy**   (pronounced *ignomy*) humiliation.

208 **sentence**   judgement (also the meaning of *doom*, 209).

210 **remit** withdraw, refrain from punishing.

211 **removed** moved far away (as in 1:73 where Satan seems to regret what Belial here welcomes: their distance from God).

212 **us not offending** us if we do not offend (a Latinate construction).

213 **whence** therefore.

215–19 Belial suggests that their *essence* or pure nature gives grounds for hope: either it will purge off Hell-fire (as God is supposed to at 141), or it will become used to it (*inured*) and more like it in temperament and substance (*conformed/In temper and in nature*). Although this *conforming* would be a degeneration (see page 14), do you find his attitude more positive than Moloch's?

219 **void** empty.

220 Belial here is confusing the entire value system of creation as Satan did at 1:160 and 4:110 (see Interpretations pages 165–6).

224 Another chiasmus; their *lot* will not be happy, but need not be the worst evil *(ill)*.

Mammon advises building in Hell: Lines 229–83

Moloch, Belial, and Mammon have been described as 'the general, the lawyer, and the industrialist', the last being a particularly apt description of Mammon, who was introduced to us in 1:678–88 as a materialist even in Heaven, and who directs the mining for Pandæmonium. The second half of his speech encourages the angels to *build in Hell* (1:751), which may reflect a good desire to imitate Heaven (see Interpretations pages 168–9), or an evil desire to confuse good and evil, light and darkness (as Belial did in 2:220). The first part of his speech, after a quibbling philosophical introduction, does consider the unspoken question behind the debate: should they ask to return to Heaven? His answer (see Interpretations pages 168 and 176) is to sneer at the humiliation this would involve them in (a humiliation which Adam and Eve will be prepared to accept) using words which recall Milton's own dislike of monarchy (for example, *while he lordly sits*). Find also words which make their stay in Hell seem rather impressive and even Puritan; for example, *Hard liberty, Our own good, Useful*. What are the truths such words conceal?

229 What is the effect of the lack of exordium?

229–33 Mammon first dismisses the hope of dethroning God as being contrary to fate, which as usual in Hell is placed above God; it will only happen if chance or Chaos ruled the universe, which they do not.

234–5 Since he has dismissed the *former* hope (of dethroning God), the *latter* hope (*regain* their lost rights to Heaven, 230) should also be dismissed, because they could have no place in Heaven if they did not first dethrone God.

236 **bound** boundary.

237–46 **Suppose he... servile offerings** these lines may recall Milton's bitterness in 1660, when England gave up its new-found liberty and restored the monarchy. Charles II did *publish grace to all* by issuing a general pardon which included an expectation of future obedience (*on promise made/Of new subjection*); see headnote.

239–40 **with what eyes could we/Stand** how would we have the face to stand?

243 **Forced hallelujahs** enforced words of praise (such as the blessed sing in Revelation 19:1).

244–6 **breathes... servile offerings** gives off the perfume of the heavenly food (*ambrosia*) we present to him (though in the description of Heaven in the next book, the ambrosia comes from God, see 3:135). Mammon is 'packaging' the worship of God as slavish; compare what Satan says about it in his soliloquy (Interpretations page 176; see page 162 on 'packaging').

249 Note how this 'imaginative construction' of their return ends in the word *hate*.

249–54 **Let us not... ourselves** let us not seek our former heavenly state of splendid slavery (*vassalage*), which is impossible to obtain by force, and too humiliating to obtain by God's consent, but live independently from our own resources.

254 **vast recess** euphemism for Hell; compare Moloch's name for it at 2:58.

256–7 **Hard liberty, easy yoke** difficult liberty (is preferable to) easy responsibilities. Is Milton putting much of his own preference for liberty into Mammon's mouth (see Interpretations page 168)? Beëlzebub dismisses this *liberty* (2:316–21). The *yoke* (burden) may be meant to recall Jesus's offer to the heavy-laden: 'For my yoke is easy' (Matthew 11:28–30).

260 **We can create** main verb; the preceding adjectives (*Useful... adverse*) show what kind of positive *things* can be created from

their opposites, so demonstrating the angels' power to overcome difficulties like the Puritan colonists of the New World.

262 **labour and endurance** this Puritan plea for *labour and endurance* is somewhat contradicted by his next promise of comforts.

264 **Sire** lord.

266 **majesty of darkness** see Psalm 18:11–13: 'his pavilion round about him were dark waters and thick clouds... The Lord also thundered in the heavens.'

268 **Mustering** gathering together.

271 **Wants not her hidden lustre** does not lack (archaic meaning of *want*, as at 272) her hidden brightness; the feminine pronoun recalls 1:685–7, where mining is a kind of rape.

275 **elements** materials out of which we are made (instead of the angelic ether; see note to 2:139). Devils were supposed to be made of Hell-fire, and Mammon, like Belial in 2:215–20, welcomes this transformation.

276 **temper** temperament (the balance of the 'humours' in seventeenth-century science).

277–8 **needs remove... pain** necessarily kill those too sensitive to pain. In fact Satan, who feels their woe most keenly, does not die but degenerates.

280 **order** see Interpretations page 178 on the chaos this conceals.

281 **Compose** organize.

The response of the fallen angels and description of Beëlzebub: Lines 284–309

The relieved applause of the angels, on hearing two of their princes advise peace after the storms and *thunder* of their recent battle, is clearly not what Satan wanted or expected to hear. His motion had only invited contributions on the method of continuing their war with God, but Belial and Mammon have advised ending the war altogether. That Beëlzebub and Satan now combine to reverse the angels' 'decision' demonstrates how false are promises of free choice in Hell. The passage also gives us our first description of Beëlzebub, who like Satan (1:593) retains a strong resemblance to the unfallen archangels (see Interpretations page 177).

286–90 This epic simile, comparing the applause to the sound of a dying storm, is discussed in Interpretations page 160. The deep-sea music (*hoarse cadence*) after a storm soothes the overtired (*o'erwatched*) sailors in their small boat (*bark... Or pinnace*); the fallen angels too are recovering from a storm.

292 **field** battle.

294 **Michaël** the archangel who led God's army (6:250).

295 **Wrought still** continued to work away.

296 **nether empire** lower kingdom (dismissed by Beëlzebub, 378).

297 Compare 221–2 above.

298 **In emulation opposite** in rivalry and in opposition (like the temples to the pagan gods described in 1:400–3).

301 **Aspect** expression.

302 **A pillar of state** a main support of the state.
on his front engraven (lines) etched into his forehead.

303–4 The qualities of thoughtfulness, care for the ordinary subject, and the ability to advise princes, are half-personified as presiding over his mind – or at least his features. His intelligence is clear from his speech.

305 **sage** wise.

306 **Atlantean** like those of Atlas (the Titan who supported the sky as a punishment for rebelling against Zeus). Again his appearance, not his nature, is being described.

307 **look** gaze (presumably stern).

Beëlzebub's proposal and the angels' response: Lines 310–89

Beëlzebub begins by demolishing the peaceable arguments of Belial and Mammon, echoing their words contemptuously (*thus far removed, peace, doing,* and *suffering*) and dismissing their hopes as fantasies (*dream, projecting*). He is closer in spirit to Moloch's understanding of Hell as a *dark opprobrious den of shame*, and also urges the necessity of seeking *revenge*. However (and here he does agree with Belial and Mammon), he does not see any point in a *dangerous expedition* against Heaven itself, and so proposes the plan which Satan had introduced at 1:650–6: to go to Earth and corrupt Mankind (see page 12). How does he inflame the fallen angels' jealousy and appeal to their cowardice?

310–11   Note the flattering exordium, violently reversed at 313 with the prominently placed *Princes of Hell* (sneering at their *nether empire*, 296).

312   **style**   title.

317   **dungeon… safe retreat**   with which previous speakers would you associate either of these descriptions of Hell?

318–19   **Beyond his arm, to live exempt, in new league**   three phrases which ironically elaborate on the supposed *safe retreat*: out of God's reach, outside his law, or in a confederacy *against* his rule.

320   **but**   introduces what he really thinks (that God has *doomed* or condemned them permanently).

321   **thus far removed**   a contemptuous quotation from Belial's speech (211).

321–2   **bondage, curb**   words used for restraining animals. What does this imply about the fallen angels?

322   **reserved**   preserved (he suggested in 1:149 that they were enslaved to serve God).

324   This recalls biblical phrases about the universal presence and the eternity of God, from Romans 8:39: 'Nor height, nor depth… shall be able to separate us from the love of God,' and Revelation 1:11: 'I am… the first and the last').

327   **His empire**   contrasting with *nether empire* (296) and *growing empire* (315).

327–8   **iron sceptre, golden**   harsh or mild rule (see Revelation 2:27: 'he shall rule them with a rod of iron').

329   Why do we sit here scheming? (*Projection* was associated with the delusive science of alchemy; see also *dream*, 315.)

330   **determined**   ended (from Latin *terminare*: to terminate).
       foiled   frustrated (also following *war*).

331–2   **terms… sought**   terms for peace have been neither offered (*Vouchsafed*) by God nor *sought* by us. This is said against Mammon's proposal at 279.

333–4   **custody, stripes, arbitrary punishment**   all words suggesting penal injustice (imprisonment, whippings, wilful punishments).

336   **to our power**   to the limit of our power.

337   **Untamed reluctance**   uncontrolled resistance.

338–9   **how the Conqueror least/May reap his conquest**   a chiasmus (pivoting on *may* because *least* and *reap* echo each other's vowels) suggesting how the angels can reverse God's plans, or at least frustrate his sadistic enjoyment; compare 1:164 where Satan speaks of *perverting* God's ends.

340 **doing, suffering** Beëlzebub takes up Belial's distinction (199), but insists that now the *doing* is all on God's side, and consists in inflicting *suffering* on the fallen angels. All they can do is to prevent him rejoicing in it (compare 371 below).

341 **Nor will occasion want** nor shall we lack occasions (are these to be military ones?).

346–7 Since Satan was expelled *before* the creation of the world and Man, Milton invents this heavenly rumour about its future occurrence (*prophetic fame*) in order that Satan should be informed about them; see also 1:651–4 and Argument to Book 1.

347 **seat** residence.

348 **about this time** the world must have been created during the nine days Satan and his angels have been lying in the fiery lake, because Satan makes a journey to it at the end of Book 2.

349 **like to us** both angels and humankind are made in the image of God; see Psalm 8:5: 'Thou hast made him a little lower than the angels, and hast crowned him with glory and honour.'

352–3 **oath,/That shook** from Isaiah 13:12–13: 'I will make a man… Therefore I will shake the heavens', though if Beëlzebub heard the oath why does he mention the rumour?

354 **Thither… thoughts** let us concentrate our thoughts on that place.

355–6 **mould/Or substance** form or material (see 139 above).

356 **how endued** supplied with what qualities.

357 **attempted** attacked (Fowler notes the pun on *tempt*, the method actually chosen).

359 **Arbitrator** judge. The fallen angels always manage to avoid calling him 'God'.

360 **exposed** note how the word is itself *exposed* at the end of the line.

362 **who hold it** those who tenant it (Adam and Eve).

364 **onset** attack; he suggests three methods: devastation, expulsion, and corruption.

367 **puny habitants** weak inhabitants (with a pun on its archaic meaning: newborn).

368 **Seduce them to our party** persuade them to betray God and join us. (Satan will do this by enticing them to eat the fruit of the forbidden tree, but at this point only the policy, not the precise plan, has been formulated.)

369–70 **with repenting hand/Abolish his own works** God nearly does

do this with the Flood, according to Genesis 6:7: 'I will destroy...
both man, and beast,... for it repenteth me that I have made
them.'

371–2   **interrupt... confusion**   spoil his triumph at our fall, the aim
which Beëlzebub had given them in 337–40. He substitutes *our
joy... In his disturbance*, the familiar policy of frustrating God which
Satan introduced in 1:162–5.

373–4   **darling sons/Hurled headlong**   God's new children, humankind,
will be expelled from Paradise exactly as Satan was from Heaven in
1:45; why does Milton repeat the phrase, and what do you feel
about humankind suffering precisely the same fate as the fallen
angels?

374   **partake with us**   share our punishment.

375   **frail originals**   Adam and Eve, the weak parents of the rest of
Mankind. Beëlzebub hopes all humankind will be punished for
Adam's *original* sin, as indeed they are, for eating the fruit *Brought
death into the world* and Eve in particular was *cursed* for this (1:3;
see page 13).

375–6   **faded, Faded**   at one of the saddest moments in the poem, when
Adam sees that Eve has eaten the fruit, he drops a garland he had
made for her, and *all the faded roses shed* (9:893); this is when decay
first enters Paradise.

378   **Hatching**   plotting (with a sneer at Mammon's plans for
improving Hell, 273).

379–80   **first devised/By Satan**   Satan first suggested it to the angels in
1:650–6, though we can suppose he has discussed it in more
detail with Beëlzebub.

382–3   **confound... in one root**   ruin the entire race by ruining its
ancestor (Adam).

383–4   **Earth... and involve**   we see the beginning of the mingling of
Hell with Earth at the end of Book 2, when a bridge is built
between them along which Sin, Death and the devils pass.

384   **spite**   a word particularly associated by Milton with Satan's
revenge misdirected on to the easier target of Mankind.

386   **His glory to augment**   to increase God's glory (by forgiving and
restoring fallen humankind).

387   **states**   ranks in Parliament.

389   **They vote**   is the democracy an illusion, or are they really free
and united?

Beëlzebub asks for volunteers and the angels' response: Lines 390–429

Beëlzebub expresses his pleasure at the angels' decision by flattering them, and by elaborating on the pleasures in store for them in Earth (see Interpretations page 163 on his advertisement of Earth's amenities). His request for a volunteer mimics God's similar request in Book 3 for a volunteer to save humankind:

'Say heavenly powers, where shall we find such love,
Which of ye will be mortal to redeem
Man's mortal crime? ...'
He asked, but all the heavenly choir stood mute   (3:213–17)

Then Jesus offers to make the journey to Earth, because only he has sufficient love to accept Adam's punishment of death in his place. Like God, Beëlzebub mentions the qualities necessary for the journey, though in his case they include not *love* but *strength*, *art*, *evasion*. Is he exaggerating the difficulties of the journey and if so, why? Do you think Satan is genuinely of *highest worth* (429) in daring to go?

391   **Synod**   council.
       like   (you have judged) according to your true status as gods.
       Contrast his previous exordium (313).
394–5 **ancient   seat, bright confines**   their birthright, the bright
       regions of Heaven.
395–6 **neighbouring, opportune**   their proximity to Heaven might
       offer opportunities for attack.
397   **mild zone**   temperate region.
398   **not unvisited**   a double negative, therefore *visited*. In fact the light
       on Earth comes from the sun, not Heaven (though all light imitates
       the divine light).
399   **orient**   from the east (or more simply, brilliant).
400   **Purge**   Beëlzebub is applying Belial's description (2:141) of how
       God would cleanse himself of Hell, to the angels themselves.
404   **Sufficient**   fit.
       tempt   attempt.
       wandering   see Interpretations page 178.

405 **unbottomed** limitless. Chaos, which would have to be crossed to reach Earth, has some of the associations of outer space.

406 **palpable obscure** almost touchable darkness (compare 1:63 and see page 12).

407 **uncouth** unknown and rough.

408 Note the concentration of unstressed, flapping syllables in *indefatigable* (undaunted; see Interpretations page 158).

409 **abrupt** precipitousness (see Satan's fall 2:933); the rhythm evokes the sense.

409–10 **arrive/The happy isle** arrive at Earth (here associated with the Islands of the Blessed of Greek myth).

412 **stations thick** pickets close together (like stars, suggests Broadbent).

413–15 **Here he had... suffrage** he will need here the ability to look around him and we will need careful choice in our election.

416 **weight** responsibility.

418 **suspense** suspended.

419 **second** support.

420 **mute** silent; its position at the end of the line is repeated in 3:217 (see headnote).

424 **Heaven-warring** warring on Heaven.

425 **So hardy as to proffer** so daring as to offer to go.

428 **monarchal pride** kingly pride, contrasting with Jesus's *meek* offer in 3:266.

Satan offers to journey to Earth: Lines 430–66

We see two sides to Satan here: he is undoubtedly heroic and self-sacrificing in undertaking a journey with difficulties he anticipates fairly accurately (see 2:629–1055); and yet he also seems manipulative, making use of his heroism to consolidate his position (445–56). When praising himself, his grammar is very convoluted, suggesting a dubious argument. From 456 he gives the angels new instructions, which show his awareness of their different desires; some are to retain their military occupation and guard Hell; some are to try to make it more comfortable; no-one is to accompany him. Having taken the burden of revenge, he has left them to *peaceful sloth* (227). Why does he end so abruptly?

430 **progeny** race.

  empyreal thrones heavenly kings.

431 **demur** doubt.

432 **undismayed** he is flattering them; see 2:422.

432–3 **long is... to light** in *Aeneid* VI the Sibyl explains that the journey down to the underworld is easy, but it is extremely difficult to get back.

434 **convex of fire** dome of fire (as at 1:298 and 2:635).

435 **Outrageous to devour** immoderately hungry to eat us (see the illustration on page 161).

  immures walls.

436 **Ninefold** the Styx circles Vergil's underworld nine times, but Satan finds at 2:645–6 that only the gates of Hell have nine thicknesses (*ninefold*) of which only three are of the fabulous impregnable rock *adamant*.

437 **egress** exit.

438–41 **void profound, Wide gaping, abortive gulf** phrases which support Belial's nightmare vision (2:150) of a *wide womb of uncreated night*. How do these additional body words (*gaping* or yawning, *abortive*) suggest undoing of creation and dissolution? In fact Chaos will turn out to be anything but a void.

439 **unessential night** formlessness and darkness of Chaos (see pages 11–12).

442 **scape** escape.

443 **what remains him less** what remains for him apart from.

445 **ill become** not be worthy of.

447–50 **if aught... attempting** if anything judged of public importance, should, because of its difficulty or peril, deter me from performing it.

451–6 **and not refuse... honoured sits** why do I agree (*not refuse*) to reign if I will not accept danger as well as honour? He who reigns must expect as his *due* more danger (*hazard*) for every increase in honour. Is Milton deliberately making Satan oversubtle and convoluted?

457 **intend at home** occupy yourselves as if at home.

461 **respite, deceive, slack** give a break from, cheat, or lessen the pain. How do you see this task?

462 **ill mansion** evil place where they must remain (from Latin *manere*, see Note to 1:268).

  intermit no watch set an uninterrupted watch.

The conclusion of the council: Lines 466–505

Although Milton does give the angels some negative aspects here (their disinclination for danger, or their idolatrous worship of Satan), he also praises them. Satan's unselfishness (481–2), and their general unity (497) contrast unfavourably with human behaviour, and even when men show an occasional virtue, they should remember that even devils can do as much, and curb their pride in themselves. The same point was made about the building of Pandæmonium (1:695). Should we really admire these aspects of the fallen angels? The idea that they have become devils, a word used of them for the first time at 496, united in an organized campaign of tempting humans (505) is medieval, and perhaps a bit folksy. You may prefer to believe Milton means it allegorically: the *hellish foes* (504) are inside our own minds.

466–7	As in a Parliament, a king's rising signifies the end of the session and so *prevented all reply*.
468	**from his resolution raised** their courage raised by his resolute example.
470	**erst** before (when there was a chance they might be accepted).
472–3	**winning… earn** earning the reputation (for courage and self-sacrifice) simply by offering to go; Satan made a similar link between *honour* and *hazard* at 453.
473–5	**they… Forbidding** they were as afraid of his disapproval as of the journey.
478	**With awful reverence prone** bending low with awe and reverence.
483–5	**lest bad men… with zeal** which should prevent bad men from boasting of their superficial achievements (which are stirred by the desire for glory) or their industrious virtue (*zeal*) which – below the attractive surface – promotes their secret ambitions.
486	**doubtful consultations** problematic issues raised by the debate.
488–95	Epic simile comparing the change in the angels' mood to a change in the weather: stormy in the morning (488–91), sunny in the evening (492–5).
489	**Ascending** coming from the mountain.
490	**louring element** frowning sky
497	**Firm concord** faithful agreement.

498–9   In spite of being rational, and having the hope of God's mercy,
        because they live after Christ's birth, when the angels proclaimed
        peace on Earth (see Luke 2:14 and page 13).

501   **levy**   raise up.

502   **Wasting**   destroying, laying waste.

503–4   As if we did not have enough (*enow*) foes already from Hell, which
        might persuade us to unite with one another.

Games and arts in Hell: Lines 506–69

The debate ends with the kind of ostentatious ceremony Milton
might have associated with monarchy. We are then offered a relaxing
episode after the intensity of the debate: first (a) a description of
athletic games (528–46, a traditional episode in epic narrative; see
Interpretations page 151); then (b) the sorrowful singing of an epic
about their own situation (546–55), and then (c) a philosophical
debate (555–69). Do you admire these activities, as examples of the
fallen angels' culture and resourcefulness? Or do you pity them as
futile, self-deceptive, expressing a lack of purpose and direction? It
may help you to list words suggesting falsity and imitation (for
example, *alchemy* 517, *Vain, false* 565) and words suggesting the
wandering and restless characteristic of Hell (for example, *in
wandering mazes lost* (561); these are discussed in Interpretations page
178). How much are they following Satan's advice to find a *cure or
charm* (460) for their pain?

506   **Stygian**   underworld (the Styx was the river which encircled the
      Greek underworld).

508   **paramount**   overlord.

509–10   **nor less/Than**   as great as (but under the inverted value-system of
        Hell, to be the greatest is to be the worst; see 29–30).

511   **imitated**   artificial and spurious, but perhaps also revealing
      Satan's persistent memory of Heaven, as described in 3:583.

512   **globe of fiery seraphim**   a sphere of that group of fallen angels
      originally connected with fire (from Hebrew *seraph*, meaning to
      burn), imitating God in 3:583.

513   **emblazonry**   heraldic decorations
      horrent   bristling (see Note to 1:224).

514–15   They proclaim the result of their session to the lower angels who were not present at the *secret conclave* (1:795), explaining it by heralds (518).

517 **alchemy** alloy used in cheap trumpets (as Broadbent observes, in I Corinthians 13:1 even the 'tongue of angels' becomes 'sounding brass, or a tinkling cymbal' if it lacks love).

520 **acclaim** shouted applause.

522 **presumptuous** unduly confident, arrogant.
rangèd in ranks.

523 **Disband** are dismissed.

526 **Truce** peace (see headnote on *wandering restlessness*).

a) Athletic games: 528–46

528 **sublime** raised up.

529–38 The *Olympian* games in honour of Apollo (the *Pythian* god) would also have comprised races (528–9 – though not in the air) and horseback and chariot races (531–2), though the tournaments (532) are more associated with medieval games.

529 **contend** compete.

530 **fields** contests.

531 **shun the goal** avoid hitting the turning post in chariot races.

532 **fronted brigads** teams of warriors facing one another.

533–8 Epic simile comparing the games to stormy skies, thought on Earth to precede political disturbance for *proud cities*; see also the *disastrous twilight* of 1:597.

535 **van** front rank, vanguard.

536–8 The clouds appear like knights who ride (*Prick forth*) towards each other until enclosed by the masses of the opposing cloudy army; the lightning (which makes the whole sky or *welkin* burn) looks like their pointed lances.

539–41 They tear up hills with the more dangerous rage of Typhon. He is the hundred-headed Titan mentioned at 1:199 who, with his brothers, hurled hills at Zeus in revolt (see Interpretations page 149). His name means *whirlwind*. The good angels also tore up hills when enraged by the rebel angels' cannon (6:644–5).

542 Beginning of an epic simile comparing the fallen angels to Hercules (*Alcides*) who, according to Ovid (*Metamorphosis* 9), was presented with a poisoned (*envenomed*) robe on his return from *Oechalia* when he had killed King Eurytus. Unable to remove it, and maddened with pain, he tore up pine trees to make his own funeral pyre, and threw the innocent *Lichas* (545), who had brought it, from Mount *Oeta* into the *sea*.

b) Music and song: 546–55

549   **hapless**   unlucky; note the number of words here with this meaning.

550   **By doom of battle**   by judgement of battle (and therefore unjust).

550–1   **and complain... chance**   they lament that fate (the deterministic force they have substituted for God) has made the possession of virtue or strength a matter of chance. In fact, God protects *Free virtue*, including theirs (see Interpretations pages 168 and 176).

552   **partial**   prejudiced in their favour, and also 'written in parts' (Fowler ed. of *P.L.*).

554   **Suspended Hell**   riveted the attention of the inhabitants of Hell, and also interrupted their pain, as Orpheus's song had suspended pain in the underworld (Vergil *Georgics* iv 481–4, Prince); music was given the same power at 1:556–9.

c) Philosophy: 555–69

556   Eloquence charms the soul, as music charms the senses; both therefore provide the *cure or charm* which Satan had commanded them to find at 460, though there seems an element of self-deception in both.

559–61   They first discuss the philosophical conflict between God's *foreknowledge* or plan (*providence*), which appears to rob his creatures of *free will*. Since the fallen angels prefer to be fatalistic (see 550–1 above and headnote), they find no way out of the problem, and keep repeating words (see Interpretations page 178 on *wandering*).

562–5   This moral discussion concerns Stoic *apathy* or rejection of all *Passion*, including *happiness, misery,* the desire for *glory,* and the dread of *shame.* This philosophy has its nobility, but one can imagine it appealing merely to the *peaceful sloth* (227) of the fallen angels. Milton, brought up in the Christian tradition of salvation through suffering, rejects it as *Vain wisdom.*

566   **sorcery, charm**   as at 556 above these words recall Satan's instructions to the angels at 460 (see headnote); to discuss philosophy without allowing it to change behaviour cannot *cure* their situation, but it can *charm* it.

568–9   Because their hope of finding real relief is false (*Fallacious*), their willingness to endure pain (*patiènce*) or to harden their hearts (*th'obdurèd breast*) can only protect them *for a while* (567). The strength and hardness associated with *arm*, *steel*, etc., suggest both Milton's respect for Stoic patience, and his preference for the patience of the suffering and compassionate Christ.

The exploration of Hell: Lines 570–628

The final occupation which the angels give themselves is to explore Hell. How much do you admire, and how much pity them as they confront the full horror of their situation? Do they seem to be surveying rather than experiencing the pains of Hell? Notice words which continue the search for a numbing effect, such as that offered by music or philosophy (for example, *sweet forgetfulness*, 608). The infernal geography is taken not only from epic literature (particularly Dante's *Inferno* xxxi–xxxiv, where there is also an ice-landscape), but also from actual travellers' accounts. But Milton has given it a characteristic emotional dimension. Because he followed St Augustine in conceiving of evil as the negation of goodness and life, Hell is a place of perversions and anti-life. Its creations are distortions, monsters; its language is full of oxymorons and paradoxes (*Where all life dies*); and the damned live only to suffer and be tantalized by their experience of deadness and numbness (see page 167). Once again physical and emotional words are mixed together (for example, *region dolorous*, 619), and again the angels find *No rest* (618). Can you find emotional equivalents for these physical tortures (for example, the gnawing of remorse and regret)? See Interpretations page 152 where the passage is compared with one from Vergil supplied in the Appendix.

570	**gross**	keeping close together.
572	**clime**	region.
574	**flying march**	they travel by wing (though possibly by foot as well).

575–81   The names of the *four infernal rivers* are taken from *Aeneid* vi; Milton translates them, for *Styx* derives from *hate*, *Acheron* from *woe*, *Cocytus* from *wailing*, and *Phlegethon* from *flaming* (Prince). All therefore suggest and incite evil (*baleful*) emotions, even *Phlegethon*, which is flowing (*torrent*) with rage as well as fire.

582   **Far off**   Lethe does not empty itself (*disgorge*, 575) into the lake.

583 **Lethè** means *forgetting*. To drink it would intensify the numbing effect of the music (586 is very like 1:558), or of Stoic philosophy just described at 2:568–9, so *the damned* will be tortured by being denied it (605–14).

584 **labyrinth** maze, suggesting a slow-moving river delta. Why is this emotionally appropriate for *forgetting*?

587 **flood** river.

588 **beat** beaten.

590–1 **gathers heap... ancient pile** the unthawed snow and hail piles up like an ancient ruin. Milton may be remembering here the genuine description of polar exploration written by the sixteenth-century traveller, Sir Hugh Willoughby.

592 **gulf profound, Serbonian bog** the infernal snowfields are not frozen but form a yielding pit, like the *Serbonian* bog in the Nile delta (near the city of *Damiata* and south of *Mount Casius*) which, according to the explorer Sandys, looked deceptively like dry sand and so trapped 'whole armies' (Verity ed. of *P.L.*). How can this comparison be read (as an epic simile) on two levels?

595 **frore** freezing (this paradoxical cold fire is typical of Hell).

596 **by harpy-footed Furies haled** dragged by claw-footed goddesses (the Furies came from the underworld to enact vengeance in Greek myths).

597 **revolutions** repeated times.
  all the damned is Milton writing of the human souls who will be tortured in Hell, or the fallen angels themselves, whose *ethereal warmth* (601) will feel cold acutely (as they must when they become snakes, which they suffer at regular intervals; 10:575)? Whoever it is, it seems to be in the future.

598–9 This *bitter change* from cold to heat to cold is accentuated by the chiasmus (see Interpretations page 164).

600 **starve** be numbed or 'dead' with cold. Again there seems a parallel with the numbing effects of music and philosophy (see Note to 583).

601 **ethereal warmth** the celestial fire from which spirits and souls are made.

604 **Lethean sound** the cold and hot regions appear to be divided by a narrow stretch (*sound*) of the river Lethe, over which the *damned* will be ferried. This passage still seems to be set in the future.

605 **augment** increase.

610 **fate withstands** their fate (punishment) prevents them from drinking from Lethe.

611 **Medusa** to see *Medusa*, the worst of the *Gorgons* (female monsters with claws and snakes instead of hair), would turn one to stone, again a numbing image.

613 **wight** person.

614 **Tantalus** mythical king condemned to stand in the underworld river Cocytus, whose waters fled from his thirsty lips.
Thus roving on after the passage set in the future (596–614), we now return to the present and the exploration of Hell.

616 **aghast** appalled.

618–19 See headnote for the philosophical and emotional geography here.

621 A line beginning with three dragging spondees (see Interpretations page 158).

622–3 Does this line contradict Milton's repeated insistence that only Satan or Man, not God, can create evil (see page 14)? Or do you feel this landscape is *only good* because it is an instrument of just punishment?

625 **prodigious** unnatural.

627 Than those inadequately suggested by fables or one's own fears.

628 **Gorgons, Hydras, Chimèras** fantastic monsters; for *Gorgons* see Note to 611; *Hydra* was a many-headed snake; a *Chimera* is any creature composed of parts of other creatures.

Satan encounters Sin and Death: Lines 629–80

Milton's inventiveness reaches new heights in this passage, which brings to life the Christian belief that death is a result of sin (see Interpretations pages 179–80). At this point, however, neither Satan nor we know the names or understand the psychological and moral implications of these characters, and it is Satan's courage in confronting his first real challenge since his Fall which is most striking (677–80). Milton models the woman, *Sin*, on two allegorical female monsters: Spenser's Error (*Faerie Queene* I 14), also a snake below the waist, and the mythical *Scylla* (*Aeneid* iii 424), who gave birth to dogs. Such myths might suggest fear of female sexuality, though Sin herself seems to be a victim rather than an aggressor, figuratively raped by the dogs who *kennel* in her womb (658). The *other shape*, Death, emerges not from classical sources, but from medieval pictures of King Death with his spear, and from those human fears of darkness, extinction, and shapelessness which Belial had exploited in his speech. Milton intensifies the atmosphere of horror by his epic similes (see Interpretations pages 152–3, and the illustration on page 180).

630   **highest design**   ambitious purpose.

631   **Puts on swift wings**   flies fast (not a new pair!).

632   **Explores**   tests, finds the way for.

633   **He scours**   he searches.

633–4   **coast, deep**   perhaps the edge of the burning lake.

634   **shaves**   skims.

635   **fiery concave**   roof vaulted with fire (as in 1:298).
          touring high   circling.

636–42   Epic simile comparing Satan to a spice-fleet, which although actually sailing *Close* before the trade winds at the Equator (*equinoctial*), appears to be suspended in the sky. Such fleets brought spices and medicines (*drugs*) from Bengal and the Spice Islands *Ternate* and *Tidore* in the Indonesean archipelago, on the merchant route (*trading flood*) towards the South Pole, round the Cape of Good Hope, and back towards England. How many points of comparison can you find between Satan and the fleet (look at the mirage, the journey, the cargo, and its effect on the purchaser)?

641   **wide Ethiopian**   broad ocean off Ethiopia.

642   **Ply stemming nightly**   tack their way at night (as Satan is doing).

644   The walls of Hell meeting the roof which bristles with fire.

645–6   This was anticipated by Satan in 2:435–7, though he said all nine thicknesses were adamant.

647   **impaled**   fenced (but not consumed) by fire.

652   **Voluminous and vast**   with numerous heavy coils (note the alliteration).

653   **mortal**   deadly (the opposite way round from I Corinthians 15:56: 'The sting of death is sin').

654   **cry**   pack.

655   **Cerberean**   like Cerberus, the three-headed dog who guarded Hades.

656   **peal**   the baying of hounds; unending barking was one of the tortures of Dante's *Inferno*.

659–66   Epic similes comparing Sin's dogs to those associated with *Scylla* (see headnote) and Hecate. Scylla was a nymph who was made to give birth to dogs by Circe, aided by Hecate, Queen of the witches, who was supposed to ride through the air followed by dogs, and who also held a key (see 725 below).

660–1 **the sea... shore**   the straits which separate *Calabria* in Italy from the murmuring beach of Sicily (*Trinacria*). This is where Scylla was supposedly turned into a dangerous rock.

662 **night-hag**   Hecate; see Note to 659–66.

664 **infant blood**   murdered children were supposedly used in witches' spells.

665–6 The long nights of *Lapland* were thought to attract *witches* powerful enough to eclipse the moon (which supposedly *laboured* when eclipsed, though the word might also refer to its changing shape). The fallen angels were also associated with the moon and witchcraft (1:781–8), and Satan with eclipses (1:597).

667–70 **If shape... either**   it had no clear body either in shape, limbs, or material, for *substance* and *shadow* seemed to be like one another. Hell is a place of contradictions and nightmare.

668 **member**   part.

671 **Furies**   see Note to 596 above; notice the alliteration in these frightening lines about Death (671–3).

672 **dart**   spear.

673 **crown**   see Revelation 6:2: 'a crown was given [Death], and he went forth conquering'.

676 **horrid**   causing horror.

677 Satan was unafraid, but wondered what this might be. Does this show courage, or simply an inability to fear (see Interpretations page 171)?

678–9 **God... nor shunned**   he only truly valued or feared God and Jesus (who was not *Created* but begotten). Does this suggest an uncaring, nihilistic basis to his courage, reminiscent of Moloch (2:48–9)?

Sin prevents the battle between Satan and Death: Lines 681–745

We learn here of Satan's genuine feelings about these characters; note the contrast between the words he uses here (such as *execrable*, *detestable*) and the *smooth* words he uses later to Sin after 815. We are also shown aspects of his character besides courage: for example, arrogance (683) and determination (684). Death seems equally proud (as he was traditionally characterized), and there is an almost comic debate between them about who has the highest rank (Death was only born in Hell, but he believes himself king); its irony is revealed when Sin tells them they are father and son. She tells them that the real battle will be between both of them and Jesus, but the drama of this near battle makes the epic more exciting and more classical. Do you think it appropriate that Death appears (for example, at 699–700) to express God's point of view? Why does Milton consistently refuse to name Death, using instead words like *goblin* and *grisly terror*?

681	**execrable** accursed, abhorrent.
683	Your misshapen face across my way; note the arrogance in this.
686	**taste thy folly** realize it was folly by its effects.
687	**Hell-born** Satan guesses right (see 782).
691	**Unbroken** the peace and loyalty (*faith*) were whole before Satan's rebellion.
692	This shows Satan was exaggerating at 1:633.
693	**Conjured** conspired (from Latin *jurare*, meaning to swear).
696	**spirits of Heaven** he and Sin have not been punished and so consider (*reckon*) themselves still heavenly.
700	Death assumes Satan is fleeing the pains of Hell, and tells him to return faster than he came (*add wings*).
704	**grisly** causing horror.
705	**grew** because Death has no definite shape, it cannot be contained, and its growth threatens to absorb those near it (*His famine* of 847 below). Satan also grows, becoming more fiery (708).
707–8	**indignation... Unterrified** a similar contrast to 678 above, with the word describing his lack of fear again placed at the beginning of a line.
708–11	Epic simile comparing Satan to a comet which appeared in 1618 in the northern constellation of *Ophiucus* or 'serpent-holder' (suggesting he is equivalent to Death with his *whip of scorpions* 701). Comets with tails (*horrid hair*) like the *eclipse* (666) supposedly brought disasters.
712	Satan also seems to be armed with a spear.
714–18	Epic simile comparing the encounter with that of storm clouds which, like eclipses or comets, also presaged disaster (see 2:533–8). Note the onomatopoeic effects of repetitions, particularly *t*.

715   **With heaven's artillery fraught**   laden with lightning and
thunder.

716   **Caspian**   the Caspian sea was supposedly subject to
storms.

718   It was believed that thunder was caused by the crashing together of
storm clouds; see 2:538 above.

721   **but once more**   referring to Jesus' descent into Hell to
bind Satan and release humankind. He had overcome Death
by dying on the Cross; see Hebrews 2:14 and page 13.

723   **Had been**   would have been.
rung   resounded.

725   **fatal key**   the keys of our fate. Sin is the opposite of St Peter,
who holds the keys to Heaven (Matthew 16:19).

729   **mortal**   deadly.

731–4   Like Beëlzebub (1:143–52), Sin realizes that God must have
preserved Satan for some purpose, which she believes to be the
satisfaction of his derision (*laughs*; see 2:191) and *wrath*. She is
humanizing God too much, but it is true that Death and Satan
will be the instruments of God's justice towards sinners.

732   **ordained his drudge**   designated his servant.

734   Jesus will destroy both Satan and Death at 'the end'
(I Corinthians 15:24–28).

735–6   **the hellish pest/Forbore**   Death (again unnamed) did not strike.

736   **these**   these words.

738   **Thou interposest**   you interrupt and thrust yourself between
(him and Death).

738–40   **my sudden... intends**   my hand, forestalled from an immediate
blow, waits before it shows you (*tell thee... by deeds*) its purpose.

742   **first met**   Sin is so changed (now *double-formed* as a snake-woman)
that Satan does not realize he has known her before.

Sin tells her story: Lines 746–814

The incestuous relationships which Sin now describes must be read
allegorically (see Interpretations pages 179–80), as a parable of the
self-love and self-destruction of sinning, or we will feel too much
sympathy for Sin. Satan's 'marriage' with Sin and the birth of Death
creates a hellish trinity which parodies the Holy Trinity of Father,
Son, and the Holy Spirit who comes from both. Do you find the

story revolting, or tragic, or too abstract to be either? What does it reveal about the psychology of sin (for example, the presence of self-hatred as well as self-love)?

746 **portress** female gate-keeper.

748 **deemed** thought.

749–51 The *assembly* of rebellious angels (*seraphim*) is described in 5:743–907.

756–8 The goddess Athena sprang fully armed out of the head of Zeus; Eve will be made out of the side of Adam and resemble him and God (8:465–471, Genesis 2:21–22). What do such myths seem to be saying about women?

757 **shining heavenly fair** probably meant of Satan, then Lucifer (bringer of light).

761 **Portentous** ominous, unlucky (as she is).

763 **The most averse, thee chiefly** those most opposed to me, particularly yourself.

764–5 On this self-reflective mirror, see page 14. Eve (like Narcissus) also briefly falls in love with her own reflection (4:465–6).

765 **enamoured, joy** words suggesting lust.

768 **fields** battles.

770–1 **rout/Through all th'Empyrean** disorderly flight through Heaven (the *Empyrean* is the region of upper fire); see page 12 for the events alluded to here.

772 **pitch** height.

775 **with charge to keep** like Eve, Sin is given a responsibility (*charge*) by God, from which she will be tempted by Satan; see Interpretations pages 181–2 for a detailed discussion of the key.

778 **long I sat not** it was not long. Scarcely two weeks have passed since the fall of Satan, so gestation is quick.

779 **excessive** ready to give birth or increase.

780 **Prodigious** unnatural, portentous.
rueful throes penitential pains (perhaps allegorizing the remorse after sinning).

785 **Transformed** her lower (*nether*) part was *transformed* by the birth of Death into a snake's. She thus mirrors what Satan will become (9:86, 10:531).
inbred bred inside me.

787–9 The name of *Death* is given by a kind of echo, recalling the reflections in the myth of Narcissus, who was loved by Echo.

794	That rape made us the parents (of the Hell-hounds).
796–800	This process was described more fully in 656–9 above, though their hunger (which mirrors Death's) was not mentioned then. Spenser's snake-woman, Error, herself poisons and eats her canine brood.
798	**list** wish. One of the most sympathetic aspects of Sin is that she suffers others' acts rather than acting herself (though she did win Satan, 762).
801	**conscious terrors** living terrors, but also the terrors of conscience which are born from sinning.
802	**rest or intermission** Hell denies rest (see headnote to 506–69 above).
803	**in opposition** opposite but also opposed to me. The discord between the monsters would seem characteristic of Hell, but in fact they will soon form the same *concord* (497) as the rebel angels.
805	**devour** like the *repast* of the Hell-hounds, Death's devouring of Sin would be another kind of rape. The hunger of Death is traditional, and seems here to express his negative power, like a black hole (see 705 above).
806–9	As Sin is the cause of Death, in destroying her he would destroy himself (she would be his poison or *bane*). As at 775, she avoids naming God, preferring the neutral term *fate*.
812	**invulnerable** safely immortal; as she has already prophesied (734) Satan can die. This answers the question about their own immortality which the fallen angels constantly return to (for example, see 153–4).
813	**mortal dint** fatal blow.

Satan persuades Sin to open the gates of Hell: Lines 815–89

This is probably the best example in Books 1 and 2 of the cunning and hypocrisy of Satan (the *subtle fiend*). The deception in his previous speeches had always involved some self-deception, but here we know his real feelings about Sin and Death (see 681–745 and find words in this passage to contrast with words like *execrable* and *detestable* which are used there). Once he has *learned* his *lore* (that Sin has power to let him out of Hell, and that she was bound to him before being charged to guard the gates), everything he says to her will serve his purpose of getting to Earth. How many lies and contradictions can you find in his speech? Sin's speech reveals her consciousness that she will be violating duty (*due, owe, office*) by opening the gates, and her vulnerability to his flattery and promises. In the structure of the whole poem, her act is the first step in the process of the human tragedy. For the symbolism of the key, see Interpretations pages 181–2 and the illustration on page 161.

815	**lore**	lesson.
817	**sire**	father.

818–19   **pledge/Of dalliance**   sign of our mutual love-making (an extraordinary way to refer to Death).

821   **unforeseen, unthought of**   this statement (if true) would provoke Belial's scorn (204–7).

822   **to set free**   although this is not Satan's main purpose (which is to revenge himself on God), seducing humankind will in fact release Sin into the world.

825   **pretences**   intentions, claims.

827–30   Several of the words here (such as *uncouth*, meaning unknown) recall Beëlzebub's similarly off-putting description of Satan's journey (404–7).

827   **sole, and one for all**   alone and selflessly; there is courage as well as arrogance in this, but it parodies the genuine sacrifice of Jesus' *one for all*; see headnote to 2:390–429 above.

829   **unfounded**   without foundation, bottomless.

831   **by concurring signs**   by signs which substantiate the prophesy; he is right about these new details (Earth's shape and position) though we are not told what the *signs* were.

833   **purlieus**   neighbourhood (a position Beëlzebub only hoped for at 394–5).

834–6   The jealous suggestion that humankind was created to fill up the space left by the angels' expulsion (though in fact Satan himself claims to have known about humankind before the war), requires Satan to explain why humankind was not placed in Heaven: they might then have proved too numerous (*surcharged*) and strong and rebelled against God (compare with 367).

837–8   **Be this... now designed**   if God is plotting either this or anything even more secret.

842   **buxom**   yielding; compare Beëlzebub at 394–402 above. Satan is using the charms of Earth to sell his plan.

embalmed   perfumed, made balmy.

844   In *Paradise Lost* neither humankind nor nature is subject to death before Eve and Adam eat the fruit *whose mortal taste/Brought death into the world* (1:2–3).

846   Death is often depicted as a grinning skeleton.

847   **maw**   stomach.

848   **good hour**   the hour when the fruit is eaten and God betrayed.

849   **bespake**   spoke to.

850–1   **due... King**   Sin now names God in order to establish her mandate of duty (*due*) and obedience to keep the key.

853   **adamantine**   see Note to 436 above.

855   Not fearing to be outclassed by any living power.

856–7   Sin appears to have more justification for this claim than Eve will, though she too feels *thrust down* by God (9:759; see Interpretations page 179).

858   **Tartarus**   see Note to 2:69.

859   **office**   duty, responsibility.

862–3   Sin is surrounded (*compassed round*) by the horrors and sounds of her children: Death and the Hell-hounds.

864–6   Are you touched by these lines, or do you feel they express only the lonely psychology of sin?

868   **The gods who live at ease**   humankind; she has misunderstood 834–7.

869   **At thy right hand voluptuous**   this parodies Jesus' seat at the right hand of his Father, though Sin expects a sexual (*voluptuous*) dimension as well.
        beseems   is appropriate for.

871–2   **fatal key/Sad instrument**   Sin's misuse of the key is the equivalent of Eve's eating of the forbidden fruit in its moral effect: each object is a tragic *instrument* for the release of Satan, Death, and herself into human history (see Note to 725 and Interpretations pages 181–2).

873   **bestial train**   snaky tail.

874   **huge portcullis high updrew**   drew up high the huge inner grating.

875–6   **Which but... moved**   which none of the powers in Hell apart from herself could have begun to move.

877   **wards**   the projections on the key (which had *warded* against escape).

878   **massy iron or solid rock**   for the gate's mixed construction, see 645–7 above.

ease   this prominently placed word not only suggests *release* but also the moral truth that it is easier to admit than to exclude evil (see also 883–4).

883   **Érebus**   the lowest part of Hades.

883–4   **but to shut/Excelled her power**   only Jesus has power to shut the gates (Revelation 1:18: 'I have the keys of hell and of death').

885   **bannered host**   army with banners marching in open formation (*loose array*), visualizing Jesus's words in Matthew 7:13–14: 'wide is the gate, and broad is the way, that leadeth to destruction, and many there be which go in thereat: because strait is the gate, and narrow is the way, which leadeth unto life, and few there be that find it'.

Satan crosses Chaos: Lines 890–950

We now have a dramatic change of perspective, as we turn from watching Satan to seeing with his eyes the immensity of Chaos, which contrasts so strikingly with the enclosed and *vaulted* Hell. It also contrasts with the order of Heaven, and so must draw on Milton's personal experience of the turmoil of Civil War (see page 3). Should we see this as another psychological landscape? If we do, we should not forget that Milton seems to take his source (Ovid's *Metamorphoses* I 5–20) pretty literally: his Chaos is the receptacle (*womb*, 911) from which God created the world; see pages 11–12. The formlessness and disorder of Chaos shows its distance from God, and also, in a half-comic way, its wild freedom from his control (*Chance governs all* – including whether Satan gets to Earth or not). Satan's resourcefulness also makes him appear a second Ulysses crossing an ancient sea (*hoary deep*), see Interpretations page 151. How does Milton convey the difficulty of the journey (discussed in Interpretations page 157–9 on the rhythm)?

891   **hoary**   ancient (suggesting whiteness, which is immediately contradicted, in this confusing landscape, by *dark*).

894–5   **Night, Chaos**   rulers of Chaos, whose rule is an absence of rule (*anarchy*); see Note to 988 below. There is a similar paradox in *by confusion stand*.

898–902   Milton personifies the qualities of the four elements (hot/fire, cold/air, moist/water, dry/earth) as the leaders (*champions*) of four armies of *atoms*. These *atoms* are *armed* with different qualities (for example, *swift* atoms are seen as *Light-armed*) which encourages them to form different sub-groups (*factions* or *clans*), such as those which existed in Cromwell's unstable Commonwealth (see page 4).

903–4   *Barca* and *Cyrene* were cities in an area of north Africa, which the traveller Heylin said was 'all over covered with a light sand, which the winds remove continually up and down, turning valleys into hills, and hills into valleys'. The *atoms*, like sand, weigh down the *lighter wings* of the winds, like armies enlisted (*Levied*) to fight one another.

904   **torrid**   hot and dry.

906–7   **To whom… moment**   as the *atoms* keep changing their qualities, the quality to which most subscribe rules for that moment.

907–9   **umpire, arbiter**   names which reflect the absence of control of both Chaos and Chance; indeed Chaos's bad decisions confuse (*embroil*) the war (*fray*).

911   According to the Roman poet Lucretius, nature was created out of the atoms of Chaos and would eventually disintegrate into them again (Prince ed. of *P.L.*).

913   **pregnant causes**   the reasons which determine why matter takes different forms. What other words suggest that Chaos is like a pregnant woman?

919   **frith**   strait (again suggesting Chaos is a sea).

920   **pealed**   made to ring.

921–7   Epic similes comparing the noise of Chaos to that of a battering-ram used in war-time (when the Goddess of War, *Bellona*, is active) or the falling of the Earth and sky from its fixed position by some terrible catastrophe; yet this is also seen as a *small* thing in comparison with Chaos. This *mutiny* almost seems to anticipate the modern concept of 'entropy', a degeneration of the material out of which the Earth is made, though Milton imagines it happening not over billions of years, but suddenly, like a civil uprising.

927   **sail-broad vans**   wings as broad as sails (suggesting he is a boat, as in 2:636).

928   **surging smoke**   perhaps emerging from Hell-gate (see 889).

929   **spurns**   kicks away from.

931   **Audacious**   daring, defiant.

933   **plumb**   straight; see Interpretations page 158 on this line.

935–7   Satan's fall is arrested by the blast thrown out by a cloud inflamed (*Instinct*) with fire and saltpetre (used in gunpowder and thought to cause lightning and thunder), and he is thrown upwards.

938–9   **that fury... Syrtis**   the hot blast is arrested by a quicksand (named after the *Syrtis* in north Africa) which quenches it.

940   **nigh foundered on he fares**   he continues, though nearly sinking.

941   **crude consistence**   raw material.

942   **behoves... sail**   he needs both feet and wings (the tone is comic).

943–7   Epic simile comparing Satan's journey to that of another creature with both legs and wings, a *gryphon* (lion with eagle's head) pursuing the one-eyed Scythian (*Arimaspian*) thieves of his gold. What do Satan and the gryphon have in common (apart from their versatile methods of travel)?

Satan's encounter with the rulers of Chaos: Lines 951–1009

Milton's ultimate source is Hesiod's *Theogony*, which personified the attributes of nature as gods like Chaos, Erebus, and Night. Do you find Chaos and Night emerge here as real characters (see Interpretations pages 180–1)? Again there is an element of comedy; Chaos, for example, looks *incomposed* and (as Broadbent pointed out) he does not finish his sentences. They are surrounded by attributes, taken from literature (Boccaccio and Spenser) rather than nature, who are even less clearly realized. Why, for example, is it *Discord*, and not *Rumour*, who has many tongues? But the probable purpose of the episode is not to explore the theology of Chaos, but to show again Satan's cunning in presenting his journey as one that will benefit these *anarchs*. Just as he tempted Sin to open the gates, so now he tempts Chaos (can you see where he tells lies?) to give him directions. Indeed, his promises come true in one way, for he will bring darkness and moral chaos to the Earth.

954   **loudest vehemence**   an emphasis even louder than previous noises.
         plies   makes his way.

955   **Undaunted**   this has the same force as *Unterrified* (708).

959   **Bordering on light**   Satan needs to know the nearest place where the darkness of Chaos is illuminated by Heaven's light, as he knows Earth is close by Heaven.

        straight   straight away.

960   **pavilion**   ceremonial tent.

961   **wasteful**   desolate, laid waste.

962   **sable-vested**   clad in black.

963   **consort**   queen, but equal in power.

964–7   In Boccaccio's *Genealogy of the Gods*, *Orcus*, *Adès* (both personifications of Hades), *Rumour*, and *Discord* are all children of *Demogorgon*, the most ancient god (Hughes ed. of *P.L.*). See also Vergil's monsters in Appendix page 198. Do you find this chant of strange names effective?

964   **the dreaded name**   himself, in person. His name was used in magical invocations; Marlowe's Faustus uses it to invoke Mephistopheles. See Appendix, page 200.

970   **I come no spy**   this statement contrasts with how Beëlzebub explained the journey in 2:354–8.

977   **Confine**   border.

977–84   Satan begins his temptation by suggesting that God *won* Earth (*some other place*) from Chaos's territory. If Chaos agrees with this (absurd) interpretation, he should show Satan the way there, so that Satan can recover it for Chaos.

980   **profound**   deep abyss (an adjective used as a noun).

982   **To your behoof**   to your benefit.

        lost   lost to Chaos's kingdom.

982–5   **if I... journey**   if I, having expelled the intruder, restore Earth to its original chaos and your rule, I will have achieved the purpose of my present journey.

987   **revenge**   Satan's single-minded purpose contrasts with the wandering of his fellow-angels.

988   **anarch**   non-ruler.

989   **incomposed**   disturbed.

992   **Made head against**   threatened.

995–6   The repeated words in 995 and the repeated idea of confusion in 996 (to *confound* is to throw into *confusion*) express the disintegration as fall (*ruin*) is added to ruin, flight (*rout*) to flight.

996–8   **Heaven gates... Pursuing**   the pursuit by the victorious angels is referred to at 1:169–70 and 2:79.

999	**if all I can will serve** if the most I can do will help at all (though the sentence is not finished).
1001–2	Their own civil wars are diminishing their own power (*sceptre*).
1002–6	Chaos here takes up Satan's suggestion (977–80) that God's creations are at his expense. Both Hell and the universe (*heaven and earth*) were stolen from his kingdom (though again he does not finish his sentence).
1005	**golden chain** an idea derived from Homer's *Iliad* viii, 18–27, where Zeus says he can draw all things up to himself by a golden chain; this was allegorized as the 'chain of being'; see page 13.
1007	**walk** journey.
1008	**danger** to whom?
	speed succeed.
1009	**Havoc** the order to 'cry havoc' meant that *spoil* or booty could be seized. Chaos is looking forward to assimilating the ruins of the universe (compare this with 921–7).

Satan concludes his journey: Lines 1010–55

We find here more dramatic changes of perspective. First we follow Satan as he labours on towards Earth, then we look back and see Sin and Death building their bridge. Next with Satan's eyes we see *Far off* the walls and light of Heaven, embodying all he has lost. Finally, we see our own universe as if glimpsed from outer space – tiny, pure, and vulnerable – with Satan hurrying to spoil it. These shifts are not just shifts in space, but in time: Heaven was *once his native seat* in the past, Sin and Death will build their bridge *soon after when Man fell* in the future, but *he hies* to Earth in the present *cursèd hour*. Our last sight of him is of his soul, full of revenge, malice, and danger, but also *Accursed*, still impressive, and still pitiable.

1010	Satan's discourtesy shows his single-mindedness and hypocrisy.
1013	**pyramid** flame-shaped (suggesting *puri*, the Greek word for fire).
1016	**Environed** surrounded.
1016–20	Two epic similes of constricting journeys. The first compares Satan to Jason, who sailed in the *Argo* through the clashing rocks

of the Syplegades at the eastern end of the Bosphorus (*justling rocks*), in order to get the Golden Fleece. The second relates him to *Ulysses*, who by steering to the left (*larboard*) successfully passed between the rock Scylla and the whirlpool *Charybdis* at the straits of Messina between Italy and Sicily (see Note to 2:659–66).

1021–22   The repetition emphasizes Satan's difficulties.

1023   **soon after when Man fell**   Milton here anticipates 10:293–324 when, because Mankind has disobeyed God, Sin and Death are able to build a road from Hell for demons to ascend and humans to descend.

1024   **amain**   without delay.

1026   **a broad and beaten way**   a broad and much-used road, recalling the 'broad... way, that leadeth to destruction' (Matthew 7:13; see Note to 885).

1029   **utmost orb**   outer orbit of the universe, the sphere of fixed stars, which Milton imagines as being surrounded by a protective shell.

1033   St Augustine taught that one of the consequences of the fall of Adam is that human beings become much easier to tempt to do evil. The few who resist (for example, Noah) are guarded by *special grace* from God.

1037   Satan has reached the border between nature (which has light and form) and Chaos (which is dark and formless). The light comes from Heaven, not the sun, which is orbiting the Earth far within the universe; see the illustration on page 11.

1040–1   A pair of lines which parallel 1021–2, the repetition exposing the change.

1042   **dubious**   uncertain, faint (like *glimmering*, 1037).

1043–4   The image of the *weather-beaten vessel* recalls other metaphors of Satan as a ship crossing the sea of Chaos (for example, in 2:636 and 2:927), but may also be a poignant contrast with the song *Never weather-beaten sail* where the boat is an image of the soul finding port in Heaven. The *shrouds* (sails) also suggest a parallel with death.

1045   **emptier waste**   less chaotic space (though not yet true *air*).

1046   **Weighs**   hovers.

1048   **undetermined square or round**   since authorities differed on the shape of Heaven (Plato has it round, so that the Earth mirrors it; Revelation 21:16 has it 'foursquare'), Milton leaves the question open by implying it was too *wide* to tell.

1049–50   See the description of Heaven in Revelation 21.
  1052–3   Compared to Heaven, the universe looks as small as a star seen
               beside the moon.
    1054   **fraught**   laden (still like a ship).
    1055   **hies**   goes.

Interpretations

Interpreting the poem as myth or classical epic

Paradise Lost as myth

In choosing the stories of the Fall of Satan and the Fall of Adam and Eve for his great work, Milton may have felt he was choosing myth rather than history, and so giving himself much greater freedom for his pen.

A myth is an ancient fictional story embodying some central principle or answering some key question, and as it often involves supernatural characters, it can be read symbolically rather than literally. In his unorthodox religious book *On Christian Doctrine* (written while he was composing *Paradise Lost*, but remaining unpublished until long after his death), Milton drew a distinction between the kind of truth the Bible revealed about natural and supernatural characters. When we read about the natural characters we can believe what it says is history, but when we read about the supernatural, we cannot expect it to be more than 'accommodated truth', the kind of inspired poetic fables used by Moses, who supposedly wrote Genesis. Such fictionalized histories or 'myths' answer questions about our origins or our human predicament, but do so in a different way from history, because their underlying meaning is more important than their literal narrative.

Milton's myths of Satan and of humankind both answer the same question: 'If God is good, why did evil come into the world?' Milton may or may not have believed in the literal existence of Satan, but both stories demonstrate his belief that evil was not invented by God, but arises from false choices within the minds of free individuals. Milton therefore sees himself as the successor to

Moses (as he says in his invocation, 1:8), inspired by the same Holy Spirit to elaborate the myths of the Bible so as to teach an inner truth about *the ways of* God (26). However, he also saw the Bible as documenting the first part of human history as a whole, and Books 1 and 2 are full of allusions to Old Testament characters and stories. Moses' flight from Egypt after the seven plagues recurs more than once in similes, and the early history of the Jews when they were establishing themselves in a pagan land provides him with the characters of the chief devils. He added to his biblical sources his immense accumulation of classical and modern learning, so as to transform myth and history into epic (see below).

Activity

Read 1:507–21 with the Notes. How does the myth of the Titans compare with the story of the Fall of Satan, and what question about our lives does it answer?

Discussion

Greek heroes and gods seem to have benefited from exercising the qualities which landed Satan in Hell. The Titans successfully rebelled against their father Uranus, though they were in turn deposed by their children the Olympians, *So Jove usurping reigned* (514). Perhaps such stories mirror the inevitable conflict between parents and children, and answer the question as to how the new generation can grow up and achieve autonomy. In the Titans' case it was by disobedience and rebellion against their father; in Satan's case it could have been by remaining loyal to his Father. In these terms, the story of Satan is essentially a negative account of man's developing relationship with his parents, and the story of Adam, who also disobeys but is reconciled, is a positive one.

Paradise Lost as epic

Even before Milton had chosen the myths of Satan and Adam and Eve as his subject, he had determined to write an epic of some kind, and so emulate not only Moses but Homer (who wrote the

Iliad and *Odyssey* in Greek, in about 800 BC) and Vergil (who wrote the *Aeneid* in Latin, in the first century BC; see Appendix page 198). These are very long narrative poems giving accounts of the exploits of the chief heroes and gods of their national culture.

Epics of different kinds had been written since the classical past, for example Dante's *Divine Comedy* (written in Italy in the early 1300s AD), Ariosto's *Orlando Furioso*, (Italy, 1532), and Spenser's *Faerie Queene* (England, 1590). All of these influenced Milton, but he was inspired particularly by Ariosto's example to try not just to write a long narrative poem, but to copy the classical form itself in a modern language, and even to make that language more classical, so that:

> I might perhaps leave something so written to aftertimes, as they should not willingly let it die... I applied myself to that resolution which Ariosto followed... to fix all the industry and art I could unite to the adorning of my native tongue.
>
> *(The Reason of Church Government)*

Every section of these Interpretations can be related to Milton's purpose of reviving classical literature in his poem. Milton transformed the English language to make it more classical, and gave his characters the eloquence of classical lawyers. His ideas and themes are often Christianizations of the oppositions which underlie classical epic and drama. He modelled his characters on classical as well as biblical heroes. (See Charles Martindale or F.C. Blessington for a full discussion of his use of classical models; see pages 187–8 and Further Reading.) But above all Milton used his imagination to transform all these elements of epic, debate and drama into a personal vision of the battle between good and evil.

Narrative features of epic

Milton's poem is constructed like an epic, using characteristic narrative features and set pieces. Here are some which Milton adapts:
- Invocations to his Muse, or divine inspiration, as at 1:6.
- Starting the story in the middle, *in media res*. The war in

Heaven has already happened, and the temptation of man is to come, when the action begins at 1:50.

- Centring the story on heroes. Although he is evil, Satan has a good deal in common with the typical classical hero, particularly Aeneas, the hero of the *Aeneid*. Rather like Satan, Aeneas leads his defeated forces away from burning Troy, leaves most of them resting in Sicily, and virtually alone finds the site of Rome and founds a new kingdom. Moreover, in Book 1 Satan seems to have the classical virtues associated with heroes: Homer describes the compassion of Agamemnon (who, like him, sheds tears over his army's pain), the courage of Hector when faced by overwhelming odds, and the endurance and resourcefulness of Odysseus. But one can notice important differences between Satan and such heroes. For example, Satan's aim is not to found his own kingdom so much as to deprive another of his, and his heroic individuality does not serve God (as Aeneas's did) but his own pride. See page 170 below for the influence of classical tragedy on the characterization of Satan.

- Including a procession of heroes followed (eventually) by a battle. The procession is given in the passage beginning at 1:376, with a new invocation to the Muse. The battle, which has already occurred, occupies Book 6.

- Including accounts of councils. The debate in Book 2 of *Paradise Lost* is influenced by 2:50–397 of the *Iliad*, where the Greeks are debating whether to continue the war against Troy. Here too the promoters of peace (Agamemnon and Thersites) nearly carry the day, and it is only with difficulty that Odysseus stops their flight by attacking their cowardice.

- Including a description of the underworld. The most famous book of the *Aeneid*, Book 6, shows Aeneas visiting the underworld (see Appendix page 198). There he finds the four rivers mentioned by Milton in 2:574–81, and watches the games of the glorious dead (compare 2:528–46).

- Including a voyage, such as that which occupies much of the *Odyssey* (see 2:629–42, particularly noting the similes that associate Satan with the sea).

Activity

Analyse the section from *Aeneid* Book 6 which is supplied in the Appendix, page 198. How many features does it have in common with the description of Hell in 2:570–628, and are there any notable differences?

Discussion

Your observations of similarity and difference could focus on the following:

- The dream-like, almost surreal sights: for example Vergil's *shadowy giant elm* with its dream-leaves (lines 11–13), and Milton's ice landscape with its heaps of hail (589–90).
- The inclusion in both of personified emotions: for example, in Vergil, Grief and the Cares are like human beings sleeping before the gates of *Orcus* (Hell, 1–2), and Milton follows classical tradition in linking each river in Hell with a particular emotion (577–81).
- The monsters: for example, both mention the Chimera (whose body was composed of several beasts) and the snakey-haired Gorgon (Vergil 18–19, Milton 628). In Milton this links to the theme of false creativity, discussed on page 168.
- The similes: Vergil compares the numerous dead, who long to enter their final place of rest, with fallen leaves and migrating birds (35–9). Milton's Hell is not a place of rest (indeed the whole passage suggests restlessness; see page 167), though he does use the image of fallen leaves at 1:301–3. Do you think this image has a different effect in each poem?

Epic similes

Homer's epics were recited and remembered before they were written down, and Vergil retained some characteristic features of this oral tradition, notably the use of epic similes, comparisons which brought the wider world into the main story. Milton's extended similes are more like Vergil's than Homer's, because there is more than one point of correspondence between the image and its object. For example, Leviathan and the moon are compared to Satan not only because of their size but also because of their treachery: Leviathan tricks sailors into thinking him an island, while the moon presides over the hours of darkness when such things happen, and can even block out the sun in daytime. So also does Satan deceive not only his fellow angels and humankind, but himself, hiding the light of truth. These two levels of comparison mean that Satan seems both impressive and not impressive; his heroic stature is undermined.

Sometimes a comparison can also provide a contrast to the main story. The legend of Moses from Exodus, including the story of the plagues and the dividing of the Red Sea (see 1:304–13, 338–43), is a kind of mirror to the story of Satan, for Moses led the Jews out of slavery in Egypt to their own promised land, whereas Satan can only lead his fallen angels to steal humankind's promised land. The following table provides the references.

Book 1		Book 2	
Leviathan	196–209	Tempest at sea	285–90
Volcano	232–7	Clouds and sun	488–95
Moon	286–91	Hercules	542–6
Fallen leaves	301–3	Spice fleet	636–42
Red Sea	304–13	Scylla and witches	659–66
Locusts	338–43	Black clouds	714–18
Obscured sun	594–9	Bellona	920–4
Burnt pines	612–15	Griffon	943–7
Bees/pygmies/elves	768–88		

Activity

Look up two similes which involve the moon: 1:286–91 and 781–7. What is the principal point of comparison between the simile and the thing described? What is the secondary or hidden comparison?

Discussion

In 1:286–91, the principal point of comparison is size – the shield is very big – but the moon is also given negative connotations (*spotty*) and is diminished in importance by being seen through a telescope (*optic glass*). The size-shifting continues in the next few lines to 307: Satan's spear is bigger than the tallest pine tree, but the angels are compared first to leaves, and then to water-weed (*scattered sedge*), as if Milton were now seeing them through the wrong end of his telescope. Does this suggest Milton's scorn? Or does it give them the attractiveness of natural objects? Or simply suggest the dream-like world we have entered where nothing stays the same size or shape for long?

In 1:781–7, the fallen angels have shrunk to the size of tiny elves, so again the principal point of comparison is size; but the connotations are more sinister. They are like elves who dance below the moon, making wicked plans which frighten the *belated peasant*, just as the angels will soon be plotting to harm humankind. Moreover, the elves are enjoying themselves, which suggests the angels' sense of relief and recovered self-esteem.

Milton's language and style

Understanding Milton's Latinate English

Milton uses English in a very particular way, which makes him difficult to understand until you get used to his style. Partly because he wanted his poem to feel classical (see page 150), he uses English as if it were Latin, preferring long and complex sentences in which the normal word order can be upset, and often assuming you know the Latin word from which an English one has descended. In order to work out the meaning of long sentences it helps to break them down into sub-sentences, and to see how they fit together like a jigsaw; see the next activity for an example of how this can be done.

In standard English the word order tells you the grammatical construction of the sentence, so it is important to sort out what the word order would normally be. Although this is done for you in the Notes (particularly at the beginning), it is worth 'translating' every line into clear modern English until you feel able to understand it automatically.

The problem can be illustrated by comparing the simple sentence 'John liked the dog' with the sentence 'The dog liked John'. It is because of the word order that you know that John is the subject of 'liked' in the first sentence (in other words, he does the liking), and that the dog is the object (in other words, he is liked). In the second sentence the dog is the subject, and John is the object. But Milton is quite ready to say *Him the Almighty Power/Hurled headlong* instead of *The Almighty Power hurled him headlong* (44–5); but here we have a clue as to who is being hurled because Milton writes *him* and not *he*.

Milton also likes to put in sub-clauses (mini-sentences) before he gets to the subject. For example, he tells us it was *Nine times the space that measures day and night* before he gives us the main clause, *he... Lay vanquished* (50–2). Here again we have a clue to the subject, because Milton writes *he* and not *him*. It is important not to miss such clues; Milton's sentences are always precisely grammatical once you have sorted them out.

He also likes to re-order nouns and adjectives, saying for example *A dungeon horrible* (1:61) rather than *A horrible dungeon* (these are known as 'inversions'). The main poetic effects of changing the natural order of words is to give the poem its precise, emphatic beat, and to highlight important words by placing them at the beginning or the end of lines. Noticing the position of words in the line is a key to analysing the poem stylistically.

Watch out also for Milton's use of double negatives to cancel each other out. If Milton writes of the angels, *Nor did they not perceive the evil plight/In which they were, or the fierce pains not feel* (1:335–6), it means they did perceive their plight, and they did feel the pains. As usual Milton is being logical, and it is important not to miss a single clue to his meaning.

Activity

Break down the first sentence of the poem, lines 1–16, into its component sub-sentences (clauses). Why do you think Milton opened his poem with such a convoluted first sentence?

Discussion

It may help your analysis if you understand a little about the grammar here. The sentence begins with the possessive case, **Of** *Man's first disobedience*, and only reaches the main subject and verb in line 6: *Sing heavenly Muse* (the *Muse* is the subject, and the verb is *Sing*). All the other sub-sentences are attached either to *Sing* (e.g. *and the fruit*) or *Muse* (e.g. *that on the secret top*), until you reach the semicolon in line 10. The second part of the sentence has *I* as its subject and *Invoke* as its main verb, and the sub-sentences are attached to *song*.

One of the reasons for opening the poem in this way is that it echoes the opening of Homer's *Iliad*. In R. Fagles' translation:

> Rage – Goddess, sing the rage of Peleus' son Achilles,
> murderous, doomed, that cost the Achaeans countless losses,
> hurling down to the house of Death so many sturdy souls...

Both poets begin with the crucial subject of their poems: the human flaw which caused *all our woe,* though they differ about what that flaw is.

Rhythm and sound effects

Milton was fascinated by music and the stage. He liked to play the organ and sing every day. One of his first important works was a masque (a short play with music and effects) undertaken in 1634 with the encouragement of the composer Henry Lawes, and one of his last was the tragedy *Samson Agonistes*. He first conceived *Paradise Lost* as a drama, and began with Satan's soliloquy in Book 4 (see pages 174–6), written in the unrhymed blank verse of Shakespeare and his contemporaries and followers. When Milton decided that he preferred the freedom of epic form, he continued with the same unrhymed verse, a decision so unusual for a non-dramatic poem that he felt the need to justify it in his Introduction to the second edition of *Paradise Lost* (1674). As so often with Milton, his priority is to achieve greater freedom and classical authenticity:

> This neglect of rhyme... is to be esteemed as an example set, the first in English, of ancient liberty recovered to the heroic poem from the troublesome and modern bondage of rhyming.

He also explains how he will put that freedom under certain restraints: 'apt number' (referring to variation in rhythmic effect to suit the sense); 'fit quantity of syllables' (referring to the strict syllable count); and 'the sense variously drawn out from one verse into another' (describing how his verses or lines build up a long chain of meaning). The basic characteristics of Milton's poetry are therefore a regular rhythm in unrhymed lines which are all of precisely the same length, and long sentences which carry the meaning through several lines.

The excitement of the poetry, like music one can dance to, comes from the beat, and it is much easier to appreciate and understand if it is heard rather than read (see Further Reading for details of a recording). Every line of *Paradise Lost* is a **pentameter**, that is to say, it can be divided into five musical 'bars', known as **feet**. Each bar or foot consists of two syllables, of which the second is the stronger and more important (these are called **iambs**). The skill of the poet is in arranging words which naturally fit this insistent rhythm. For example, take the following line; the symbol ˘ indicates an unstressed syllable, and / a stressed one:

<pre>
˘   /   ˘ /   ˘   /   ˘   /   ˘   /
And swims or sinks, or wades, or creeps, or flies   (2:950)
</pre>

The rhythm comes from the natural stresses in the words Milton has chosen (one would not normally accent *or*). Because an alternation of stressed and unstressed syllables is natural to spoken English, it is perfectly possible for Milton, like Shakespeare, to write almost entirely in **iambic pentameters**, without sounding forced or unnatural.

Milton's iambic pentameters are stricter than Shakespeare's, but occasionally he does vary the pattern by substituting another kind of foot for one of the iambs. For example, on the difficult journey across Chaos, Satan first flutters his wings (*pennons*), and then he drops like a stone:

```
/    ˇ    ˇ    /    ˇ    /    /    /    ˇ    /
```
Flutt'ring his pennons vain plumb down he drops   (2:933)

This line contains three true iambs (can you find them?) but it begins with a **trochee**, or iamb in reverse (/ ˇ) giving a quickly moving pair of unstressed syllables, and it includes a **spondee** (two stressed syllables, / /) to suggest Satan's heavy fall. Spondees are fairly rare because they slow down the rhythm, but they are very effective when they occur. See for example line 948 in the same passage, where Milton is again conveying how hard it is to get through the varied terrain. The spondee is in bold:

```
  ˇ    /    ˇ    /      ˇ      /    /    /    ˇ    /
```
O'er bog or steep, through strait, **rough, dense,** or rare   (2:948)

Now look at the first two syllables of the previous quotation: Milton has reversed the first foot (*Flutt'ring*) to form a trochee, which has the result in this particular line of putting two unstressed syllables next to each other, like quick wing beats. This first-foot reversal is fairly common as it allows Milton to accentuate the first word in the line (such as ***Down*** *had been falling*, 935). Variations like this do of course depend for their effectiveness on the generally regular iambic pentameter.

Activity

Read Belial's imagining of how each angel might one day be chained on a separate rock, in 2:184–6, and scan it (put in the marks for rhythm, as above). What is the effect of the rhythm here?

Discussion

Interpretations of rhythm can vary, but one way of scanning these lines would be:

/ ˘ ˘ / ˘ / ˘ / ˘ /
There to converse with everlasting groans,

/ ˘ / ˘ ˘ / ˘ / ˘ /
Unrespited, unpitied, unreprieved,

/ ˘ ˘ / ˘ / / / ˘ /
Ages of hopeless end; this would be worse.

The natural stress of each word is used to build up a feeling of heavy, hopeless, endless torture, but each line has no more than the usual five feet. Milton has simply reversed the first foot of every line quoted (highlighting the *un*) and substituted a spondee for an iamb in the last line. Here *Ages* emphasizes the length of time, and *this would* dramatically sums up the whole passage and refers back to Moloch's speech (*what can be worse*, 2:85).

The passage about the journey across Chaos also contains examples of other aspects of Milton's music, particularly his use of repeated sounds. Repetition of the same sound in two different words always calls attention to itself, and can link words or even suggest the thing they describe (this is called **onomatopoeia**). Repetition of the same consonant in different words is called **alliteration**, and repetition of the same vowel sound is called **assonance**. Both are used when Satan meets the *vast vacuity* of Chaos (2:932), where two words are linked by the repeated *v* (it is a *vacuity* because it is so *vast*), while the open vowels suggest the sense of terrifying distances. An even more onomatopoeic effect is achieved when he describes a puffing cloud:

The *strong rebuff of* some tu*mult*uous cloud   (2:936)

Practically every line in this description of Satan's journey has some such effect. It is not, however, always worth looking for a meaning within the sound, as some are purely decorative, for example the exotic place names which sometimes pour out like a musical fountain (as in the parade of the gods, 1:376–521).

Activity

How are alliteration and assonance used to convey meaning in the description of the angels' applause in 2:284–90?

Discussion

The applause is muted, almost unconscious; the fallen angels welcome Mammon's shameful peace proposal because they have been reminded by Belial of the terrifying storm of God's anger. Milton suggests this by comparing the applause to the *murmur* of the sea heard not during a storm, but *After the tempest* (290), as it echoes and booms in a cave (note the assonant *o* in *hollow rocks* and *hoarse cadence*). This is contrasted with the loud *blust'ring winds* which had *roused the sea* the previous night (note the roaring and whistling sounds of the alliterated *r* and s). The angels have had enough storms, and even their applause is muted.

Imagery and description

Milton was blind when he wrote *Paradise Lost*, and it is tempting to think that this is why his images are often abstract and scholarly, and his descriptions sometimes dream-like and surreal. Half-formed images are a characteristic of his style – similes and metaphors which are half-abstract, half-visualized, always focusing on meaning (for example, Satan looks at *Regions of sorrow*, 1:65). Because his writing is a mixture of the concrete and the abstract, Milton seems able to turn inward and describe *things invisible to mortal sight* (3:55). This incidental and constant imagery often builds into chains of meaning rather as Shakespeare's does; some of these groupings are discussed below under the section on themes (see page 166).

Activity

Look at 1:230–7 and 1:670–90 and find all the words that suggest a half-formed image of Hell as a body. What is the effect of this body imagery?

Discussion

Hell had been seen in the Middle Ages as a huge mouth, where the devils eat, digest and defecate sinners as part of their torture. In the medieval manuscript depicted below, an angel holds a key to the prison within the mouth, a key which is entrusted to Sin in *Paradise Lost*.

'Hell Mouth' from the Winchester Psalter, twelfth century – note the key

In these passages, Milton uses both ends of the body's digestive process in hellish similes and metaphors; Satan flies like a volcano farting *With stench and smoke* (237), and a volcano *Belched fire and rolling smoke* (671) and seems to be troubled with dandruff (672) in the second passage. The body seems to be a female one, which the fallen angels appear to be raping (*Ransacked the centre, Rifled the bowels, digged out ribs*). Such images are disgustingly tactile; they express the degradation and perversion which runs through all the descriptions of Hell, where everything is monstrous, self-contradictory, self-destructive:

> Where all life dies, death lives, and nature breeds,
> Perverse, all monstrous, all prodigious things
>
> (2:624–5)

It must have been partly because the female body is creative that Milton used it to suggest the perverse creation of Sin – born not from God but from Satan – who becomes the mother of Death (see pages 168 and 179).

Debate and speeches

In the seventeenth century, rhetoric (or the art of public speaking) was an important part of the undergraduate curriculum, and students were expected to participate in formal academic debates. Milton excelled in this exercise, and used his debating experience in his 'polemical' literature, the tracts on social and political affairs that he produced in the 1640s and 1650s (see pages 1–2).

The purpose of a speech is not so much to describe a reality (as a narrative does), as to persuade the listener to accept one's real or pretended opinion. Accordingly the speeches of Satan and the other fallen angels often use a heightened style, which imposes the speaker's viewpoint on the audience.

Modern advertising is also deliberately persuasive and even deceitful, and Milton's angels could be said to use some of its techniques, such as 'packaging' (as when Satan makes himself sound heroic by referring to God as *Foe, Torturer, Adversary*, etc.), suggesting what life would be like without the advertised product, and offering possible futures with or without it.

Activity

In 2:390–402, Beëlzebub develops his proposal, introduced at 345, that the fallen angels should steal the Earth from humankind; he wants them to adopt this, and not *peace* (292) as their policy. Imagine Beëlzebub is an estate agent trying to 'sell' Earth as a desirable residence to the fallen angels. How does he use the methods listed above?

Discussion

Beelzebub has already 'packaged' this plan as an *easier enterprise* (345) than fighting – just as an estate agent might say that one property was more 'affordable' than another. Here he tells them of the advantages of occupying Earth. It offers fine views (394), light (397–8) and (in a mouth-watering soundbite) *soft delicious air* (400); these comforts are contrasted with the *corrosive fires* (401) of Hell. He dangles a possible future when he suggests that they might be able to move on from Earth to *Re-enter* (397) the Heaven they secretly miss.

Unlike modern advertisers, orators were expected to be virtuous, and to appeal to the nobler characteristics of their audience, which were expressed in terms of their *ethos* or moral values (such as honour), their *logos* or reason, and their *pathos* or passions. Milton knows that values, reason and feelings can all be used as agents for corruption by an orator who is consciously manipulating the truth.

Orators were also skilled at using striking words in the most effective and emphatic order, and ornamenting them with rhetorical figures of speech. The following are a selection of these features, with examples from Books 1 and 2:

• **Antithesis:** an opposing pair, as when Satan asserts it is *Better to reign in Hell, than serve in Heaven* (1:263).

• **Rhetorical question:** a question to which the answer is obvious and so not stated (e.g. *in this abject posture have ye sworn/ T'adore the Conqueror?*, 1:322–3).

• **Tricolon:** a three-part list such as *is this then worst,/ Thus sitting, thus consulting, thus in arms?* (2:163–4); this example is also a rhetorical question.

• **Trope:** an alteration of a word from its usual meaning, e.g. Hell is described as *this vast recess* (2:254).

- **Amplification:** saying the same thing in several ways, e.g. *O prince, O chief of many thronèd powers* (1:128).
- **Anaphora:** the parallel patterning of verbal structures, e.g. *whom shall we send... whom shall we find?* (2:402–3).
- **Chiasmus:** a phrase where words are virtually repeated in reverse order, e.g. *Where all life dies, death lives* (2:624).

Once you have learned to notice these features of Milton's style, you will find them throughout the text, and not just in the speeches, although in the speeches they often occur more frequently and with a particularly persuasive effect.

The speeches in Pandæmonium, like speeches in the British Parliament, are particularly formal; their structure is explained at the beginning of the Notes to Book 2 (page 108). By looking at the structure of the arguments, the persuasive devices, and the rhetorical figures used, you can better appreciate how the speakers each try to convince the fallen angels of the need to continue – or not continue – the war against God.

Activity

Look at the third section of Belial's speech (2:142–225) in which he attacks Moloch's suggestion that annihilation would be better than their present suffering. Use the modern and the classical terminology discussed above to analyse how he tries to persuade the audience to reject Moloch's point of view.

Discussion

Essentially, Belial is opposing two possible futures: one that is terrifying, appealing to the audience's secret fears, and one that is more comforting.

- He appeals to the audience's *ethos* by suggesting their punishment is a kind of martyrdom in which they suffer *ignominy, or bonds, or pain* (207; note the tricolon). This 'packages' their punishment as glorious.
- He touches their *pathos*, or feelings of self-pity, by reminding them of their fall from Heaven, using a trope when he calls Hell *A refuge* (168).

- He flatters their *logos* or rationality through suggesting reasons why inactivity might be productive, ending in a contradiction when he promises that *This horror will grow mild, this darkness light* (220).

The speech also uses several figures of rhetoric, including several antitheses or opposing pairs (such as *hope/despair*, 142–3); an oxymoron (*sad cure*, 146); alliteration and assonance (**w**ide **w**omb of uncrea**t**ed nigh**t**, 150), rhetorical questions (*who would lose*, 146); and many anaphorae or parallel constructions (*how he can… that he never will*, 153–4). It is one of the finest speeches in the poem, and Milton has to warn us that it *Counselled ignoble ease, and peaceful sloth* (227), lest we be carried away by its power.

Themes and issues

The thematic structure of *Paradise Lost* is based on the opposition between good and evil, which was discussed above on pages 11–15. This moral map is realized as geographical locations in Heaven and Hell, and the Chaos between them. In Books 1 and 2 we hear about all three, though Heaven is only glimpsed through its parody in Pandæmonium (we see it directly in Books 3 and 10).

Within this setting, characters make moral choices that introduce not only the plot of the whole poem, but also its focus on direction, its opposition of ascent and descent, which will be epitomized in the twin stories of the Fall of Satan and the Fall of Adam and Eve. In discussing such themes as Satan's ambition and pride, or his reliance on deceit and manipulation, you should always bear this framework in mind. His pride in his army could have been productive if it encouraged him to lead it back to God, and his deceit is self-destructive because it blinds him to the truth of his nature and leads him away from God. The structure can be a useful basis for note-taking on your reading, as shown in the following chart; add your own examples.

Opposition	Example
Heaven/Hell	1:255
ascent/descent	1:40, 47
good/evil	1:216–18
light/darkness	1:244–5
truth/lies	1:126
virtue/vice	2:116
love/hate	2:373–5
joy/despair	1:249–50
rest/restlessness	1:66
purposiveness/wandering	2:561
true/false creativity	1:695–9
freedom/service	2:255–7

These oppositions will help you to investigate the key themes or issues raised by the text, including the following.

Leadership and ambition

How should we place Satan? Milton's views on government and liberty are very relevant to our analysis of Satan as a leader (see pages 3–5), as are his models of heroes in Greek epic and tragedy (see pages 151 and 170).

But we should not lose sight of Satan's place in the moral map of the poem, or believe his own account of himself or of God. Is he truly higher or lower than his peers (he seems to suggest he is both at 2:24–30)? In Book 4 he admits that he is *only supreme/ In misery* (4:91–2) and indeed reveals how much he was deceiving others and even himself in his rejection of God in Books 1 and 2, and in his refusal to lead his followers through the only door back to happiness – repentance (see the discussion on pages 173–6).

The nature of Hell

Granted that it is impossible to be realistic in describing Hell and Chaos, how far does Milton succeed in giving us a sense of the terror and scope of the universe? This issue is introduced in the sections on imagery and description (see pages 160–62) and on the Gothic (see pages 182–4). But Milton also suggests that Hell is essentially a mental state, and here the oppositions listed above can be very illuminating.

For example, Hell is a state of restlessness and hopelessness (see the Activity on page 178), and the rivers of fire in 2:575–81 are reflections of the *hate* and *rage* within Satan; the monsters and chimeras express his own self-invented contradictions and deceits. Hell's inhabitants are types of vice and idolatry (see page 177). The reader is thus being shown the possibilities of creating his or her own personal Hell by moving away from goodness and truth. It is useful to compare Milton's Satan with Christopher Marlowe's Mephistopheles, who also claims that Hell is within him (see Appendix page 200).

A thirteenth-century depiction of Hell from the Baptistry, Florence

The conflicting claims of justice, freedom and equality

To *justify the ways of God to men* is Milton's stated aim (1:26), and the focus on Satan in Books 1 and 2 is clearly meant to remove the blame for sinfulness and pain in the world from God by placing it on Satan, as it will be placed later in the poem on Eve and Adam. However, Satan is such a persuasive defender of his own case that we can find all sorts of ways in which to sympathize with it rather than with God's.

In particular Milton's own passion for freedom (see pages 1–9) seems to have influenced his depiction of Satan's rebellion against authority, and made the arguments of the angels in Pandæmonium in favour of developing their own rival (and apparently less hierarchical) state surprisingly effective. On the other hand, we can argue that Satan in fact denies freedom to his followers when he manipulates the debate in Hell, and denies it to himself when he argues (as he does in a soliloquy, see page 176) that he is pre-determined to be sinful. Indeed both Belial and Mammon say that an unchanging fate (rather than a possibly merciful God) keeps them in Hell (2:197, 232).

Hell as parody of Heaven: true and false creativity

It is difficult without reading Book 3 to appreciate how Milton's Hell is a parody of Heaven, but there are many clues in Books 1 and 2 to this important theme. Satan's conception of Sin and Death parodies God's begetting of the Son and the Holy Spirit (see page 179). This 'false creativity' of Satan is mirrored in the false characterization of Pandæmonium as a place of dignity and light, adorned with gold and jewels like the City of God described in Revelation 21.

It is worth looking for ways in which Pandæmonium confuses the oppositions in the chart above. For example, it appears to rise *like an exhalation* and be a *spacious hall* (1:711, 762), but is really so low that the angels have to shrink to enter it (779); it appears to be made of precious materials but in fact the ground has been raped to reveal *treasures better hid* (688).

Truth and deceit

The opposition between true and false creativity is part of the wider opposition between truth and deceit which underlies the poem, and in particular the speeches of Satan and his fellows (see pages 162–3). One way of distinguishing what these characters wants us to believe from what Milton seems to believe is by considering how their language confuses the clear oppositions listed above. When Belial promises that one day *This horror will grow mild, this darkness light* (2:220) he may be lying, or he may be correctly predicting how embracing evil leads to the inability to distinguish truth from lies; if we eventually come to accept Satan's characterization of God as a tyrannical enemy, we will be close to accepting that opposing him is justifiable, even through the seduction of innocent humankind (2:358–76).

Interpreting the characters

In discussing the themes of the poem we will often be prompted to ask difficult questions. For example, if God created a good Heaven, why did so many angels rebel? Why did he then punish them eternally in a specially prepared torture chamber, instead of forgiving them? Why are all the angels sharing the same punishment, when some were clearly leaders and others followers?

Questions such as these are raised by Milton's biblical sources, but are made much more difficult to answer because he has made Satan and his army so real to us that we cannot help viewing them as human. Such questions are less frequently provoked by the characters Sin and Death, who are more obviously personifications of abstract qualities.

Should we read Satan and the other fallen angels as 'real' characters, or merely as representations of negative qualities such as deceit, malice and greed which we encounter in ourselves?

Satan's character

Satan has many appearances in the Bible (see Appendix page 196); for example, it is he who pauses in 'walking up and down in' the Earth to tempt patient Job (Job 1:7). His name probably means *enemy*, a name which he prefers to give to God.

When we are first introduced to him in the poem it is with the words *guile*, *envy*, *revenge* and *pride* (1:34–6). This prepares us to meet a villain, and yet when he appears he seems much more like a classical hero. We have already discussed Milton's heroic models in epic poetry; Satan displays for example the determination of an Aeneas or the ingenuity of an Odysseus in making his journey to Earth (see page 151). But he also has an affinity with the heroes of classical tragedy who, unlike Odysseus or Aeneas, often oppose the divine will, either through some mistake or through an innate flaw. For example Prometheus, the hero of Aeschylus's *Prometheus Bound*, rebels against Zeus when he gives fire to humankind, and at the opening of the play is seen chained to a rock (where his liver is daily devoured by a vulture) hurling defiance at his tormentor. His position immediately suggests Satan's at the opening of *Paradise Lost* (see Appendix page 197):

> I call upon you to see what I, a God, suffer
> at the hands of Gods – ...
> such is the despiteful bond that the Prince
> has devised against me...
> (*Prometheus Bound* translated by David Grene)

In spite of his own shock and pain, Satan cheers and encourages his army, and although you might feel he is leading them in the wrong direction, Beëlzebub seems to be right when he says that Satan's voice is their *liveliest pledge/Of hope* (1:274–5). Moreover, he is clearly superior to them in character, *by merit raised* (2:5) to his position. While they wait passively for his return, he is actively meeting danger and carrying out his plan. Indeed, when Milton sums up his character at 1:599–605, he uses the words *dauntless courage* and *remorse and passion* as well as the words *pride*, *revenge*, and *cruel*. He seems therefore to be both evil and good at the same time. How can this be explained, and is he the villain or the hero of the poem?

An engraving by James Barry depicting Satan summoning his legions, 1775

Activity

Can you find any evidence in the parts of the poem you have read for the qualities of Satan listed at 1:34–6: *guile, envy and revenge*; and for those listed at 1:599–605: *dauntless courage, remorse and passion*?

Discussion

There are several examples of Satan showing these qualities; the following are a selection.

- *Guile*: Perhaps the clearest example is the conversation between Satan and Sin. He reveals what is probably the truth at 2:745 when he says he never saw *Sight more detestable* than Sin and Death, and yet when she has explained that she holds the key to his escape from Hell, he calls her his *Dear daughter* (817) and tells her that his mission to Earth is simply to advance her and her son's interests.
- *Envy*: Here the clearest example is Satan's jealousy of humankind, expressed for example in 1:654, where Satan resents the *favour* God shows these upstarts.
- *Revenge*: Virtually every speech Satan makes can be seen as motivated by his desire to revenge himself on God for his humiliation and punishment. For example, at 1:167 he discusses what behaviour *Shall grieve him* most, and at 1:661 he seems to be speaking for all the rebel angels when he promises to continue the war, *For who can think submission*? Only Moloch expresses a similar open hatred of God.
- *Dauntless courage* (fearless courage): Satan has so little sense of fear that not even Death can frighten him (*Satan stood/ Unterrified* 2:707–8). His determination to cross Chaos in spite of its terrifying confusion is even more impressive (2:917–27).
- *Remorse and passion*: At the place from which this quotation was taken Satan even seems to regret having caused his followers to *have their lot in pain* (1:605–8). This seems to show not only a genuine affection for them, but a realization of his responsibility in wrong-doing. He even weeps for them. Do you agree with F.T. Prince, who said in his edition (see page 195) that 'this is one of the most moving touches in Milton's presentation of him as a tragic character', or do you feel this is simply another example of *guile*?

The combination of good and evil in Satan attracts our interest and our compassion; it makes him seem like a human being. In the section on Milton's religious ideas (see page 14), it was suggested that Satan has not altogether lost his original nature, for only what is good can really be said to exist. He has, however, corrupted it from its true end by replacing the love of God by the love of himself, and this pride is the essence of his evil.

His pride is clearly all-consuming: having failed to overthrow God, he will do anything to get revenge, including destroying innocent humankind simply because God loves them. And yet this pride is itself partly heroic; are not heroes essentially people who believe in themselves in spite of overwhelming odds? Is it not also his *considerate pride* (well-considered pride, 1:603) which makes him consider and help his fellow angels, even if he does so in order that they should help him achieve his ambition? Should we admire his ambition for making him determined, resourceful, brave? Or should we condemn it for making him a tyrant who is simply using his army to achieve his own ambitions and revenge? The bad is part of this good, for under the heroic qualities of courage, compassion and eloquence are egotism, pride, cunning and deceitfulness.

His deceitfulness is as significant as his pride. Practically the first thing we are told about him is that he is *Vaunting aloud, but racked with deep despair* (1:126). His words here do not reveal his thoughts; even to his *nearest mate* (192) he must put on some sort of front. Such *Vaunting* not only distracts him from despair; it is also part of his constant manipulation of others. He encourages, sneers, argues, advises, and bullies his fellow angels into obedience, while all the time promoting himself as their saviour (can you find examples of these techniques?). But does Milton mean us to think that he is also deceiving himself, and that he really believes he can revenge himself upon God?

Activity

Look closely at the speech with which Satan opens the debate in Hell (2:11–42). Make a list of all the lies he tells, and decide which ones we might suppose he himself believes.

Discussion

Satan's lies are not all of the same kind. Some seem to be only half-conscious; some are expedient half-truths designed to encourage his army; some are deliberate falsehoods designed to manipulate them. The speech opens with flattery, though it is no longer true that the angels are *Powers and Dominions, deities of heaven* (11). It is only half true to say they are *oppressed and fallen* (13), as they had attempted to oppress God first. We may imagine that Satan himself believes that Heaven is not wholly *lost* (14), although in the soliloquy quoted and discussed below he says the opposite.

It is very misleading for him to claim that *just right* and *fixed laws* (18) made him their leader, as this position was given him by God, and it is only partly true that his position is unrivalled, as he never gives them the opportunity to choose (19) a rival. It is quite untrue that Heaven is their *just inheritance* or that their defeat will make them *Surer to prosper* (38–9).

Most serious of all, he is only pretending to ask their advice, and is already limiting the question under debate to **how** and not **whether** they continue the war. In fact they do debate whether to continue the war, and even opt for peace, and it requires all Beëlzebub's powers of persuasion and deceit to make them vote for what Satan has already decided to do. This speech is therefore crucial to a consideration of the theme of freedom and equality (see page 168).

Satan's soliloquy

Most of the time we can only guess at what Satan is really supposed to be thinking, because he is so complex and deceitful, so *subtle* (2:815). However, in Book 4, when he makes his next appearance, he is alone for the first time, and he speaks his first soliloquy, surveying the Earth with envy and regret. This speech is a revelation of the 'real' Satan underneath the bluster and the lies. He begins by admitting the astonishing fact that he still loves God, and that his happiness ended when:

> pride and worse ambition threw me down
> Warring in Heaven against Heaven's matchless king:
> Ah wherefore! He deserved no such return
> From me, whom he created what I was
> In that bright eminence, and with his good
> Upbraided none; nor was his service hard.

> What could be less than to afford him praise,
> The easiest recompense, and pay him thanks,
> How due!

(4:40–8)

This underlying love of God explains why he is so set on revenge, because it explains why he cares so much that God has humiliated and rejected him. Now that he is calling things by their true names, we see that he regrets his crime, misses the *happy fields* (1:249) of Heaven, and above all feels *wrath* at his humiliation and *despair* that he has lost God's love. He continues to rail against himself:

> Nay cursed be thou; since against his thy will
> Chose freely what it now so justly rues.
> Me miserable! Which way shall I fly
> Infinite wrath, and infinite despair?
> Which way I fly is Hell; myself am Hell;
> And in the lowest deep a lower deep
> Still threatening to devour me opens wide,
> To which the Hell I suffer seems a Heaven.

(4:71–8)

Like Mephistopheles in *Dr Faustus* (see Appendix page 200), he recognizes that the true Hell is within his own mind; he made, and will always make *a Hell of Heaven* in spite of his boast at 1:255 that he can make *a Heaven of Hell*. His nature is progressing not towards creative good, but towards self-destructive evil.

At this point he confronts the unspoken question behind Books 1 and 2: should he ask God to restore him and the other angels to Heaven? He now gives his reasons for answering 'no'. The first reason is that he is too proud – though this pride mirrors Milton's own defiance of monarchy when he rejected Charles II's 'act of grace' towards the republicans and was imprisoned in consequence (see page 5):

> O then at last relent: is there no place
> Left for repentance, none for pardon left?
> None left but by submission; and that word

> Disdain forbids me, and my dread of shame
> Among the spirits beneath, whom I seduced...

(4:79–83)

His second more deadly reason is that he feels he has no choice. He feels in fact that he is 'programmed' to revolt, and so is denying free will to himself, as he denied it to his followers (see discussion of the theme of freedom on page 168). Nothing more clearly demonstrates slavery to sin than this inability to believe in free choice and imagine a better future:

> But say I could repent and could obtain
> By act of grace my former state; how soon
> Would highth recall high thoughts, how soon unsay
> What feigned submission swore; ...
> So farewell hope, and with hope farewell fear,
> Farewell remorse: all good to me is lost;
> Evil be thou my good; by thee at least
> Divided empire with Heaven's king I hold
> By thee, and more than half perhaps will reign;
> As man ere long, and this new world shall know.

(4:93–113)

The soliloquy ends in despair, a despair that expresses the best side of Satan: his recognition of God's goodness, and so his self-inflicted exile from him. This contrasts sharply with the hatred he has been expressing for God in Books 1 and 2, when God was his *Foe*, the *Tempter*, the *Victor*, and worse. If he really believed that God was evil he would not suffer to have lost his love, nor care so much about hurting him in return. It is because Satan is essentially good that he suffers, and because of his suffering that we pity him in spite of his malice.

Beëlzebub, Moloch, Mammon, Belial and the other leaders

Milton finds the names for his chief fallen angels from the Bible, though only Satan and Beëlzebub were traditional names for devils. Beëlzebub is the 'Lord of the Flies' or the 'Prince of the Devils' (Matthew 12:24). Belial and Mammon are not specific devils, but words used in the Bible to epitomize particular vices: Belial suggests depravity and licence (I Samuel 2:12–17), and Mammon suggests greed and worldly values (Matthew 6:24).

To provide names for the other captains, Milton is using an old tradition that the fallen angels, *long after* (1:383) the events described in Book 1, became the pagan gods (see headnote to 1:376–521). Moloch or Milcom was the sun-god of the Ammonites (II Kings 23:13), and the other leaders in the parade of the gods are mostly taken from the same part of the Bible, where the Jews are surrounded by, and often tempted to worship, pagan gods. Milton in fact focuses on moments when God's chosen people, the Jews, took these pagan gods into their own holy places, and purposely degraded themselves by indulging in the vices such gods encouraged: violence, lust, self-indulgence and so on.

The chiefs, however, like Satan, do retain some angelic qualities. Beëlzebub is intelligent; he alone realizes that God may have his own reasons for keeping them alive (1:143–52), and he shows *Deliberation… and public care*, and is *Majestic* (2:303–5) when he turns round the whole feeling of the debate by sneering at the fallen angels' desire to settle quietly in Hell, and introducing Satan's plan to seduce humankind in words that make it seem irresistible. Moloch retains the integrity and simple-mindedness of a true general (C.S. Lewis's word for him). He is the only fallen angel other than Satan to really feel despair because he genuinely recognizes God's superiority (2:45–50), though his speech suggests the cruelty of a god who eats human babies (1:392–6). Belial is attractive to look at, *graceful and humane* (2:109); if we were to put him in a modern setting, he would be charming a girl on his mobile, while kicking a beggar into the gutter. He is also attractive in a more subtle way, because he is the most eloquent speaker, and his evocation of our human fears of annihilation or torture ring true.

Mammon, *the least erected spirit that fell* (1:679), is also surprisingly eloquent, but his promise that *Our torments also may in length of time/Become our elements* (2:274–5) shows that he is embracing his own degradation. (See also 2:215–20 where Belial makes the same point; these passages may reflect Milton's disgust at the way the English people welcomed what he saw as the tyranny of Charles II.) It is only while the fallen angels continue to suffer pain and despair, like Satan, Moloch and perhaps Beëlzebub, that they continue to resemble the angels they once were. If you read on through the whole poem, you will see Satan gradually lose this capacity to see the truth and to suffer, as he becomes shallow and merely spiteful.

Activity

Look closely at 2:555–628, in which the fallen angels are occupying themselves while Satan is away, and find words that suggest *wandering* and *restlessness*. What reasons can you find for this state of mind?

Discussion

Heaven is changeless, but in Hell everything is in turmoil, and everyone is busy but without real direction. Milton believed that the proper end to all activities should be God or goodness, so the restlessness of the fallen angels demonstrates their internalization of Hell (see page 167). Their philosophy does not lead to a conclusion, *in wandering mazes lost* (561); this recalls Belial's description of *thoughts that wander through eternity* (2:148) without reaching back to God. The landscape they wander about in reflects the turmoil in their minds, as it is beaten by *perpetual storms/Of whirlwind and dire hail* (588–9), and they find there *No rest* (618). Compare this section with 1:65–6, where we are told that *peace/ And rest can never dwell* in Hell, and with Jesus's offer to the heavy-laden: 'I will give you rest' (Matthew 11:28). Is Satan, who seems so full of purpose, in any way as restless and without direction as his fellow angels?

Allegorical characters: Sin and Death, Chaos and Night

If the devils are something between characters and representatives of vice, Sin and Death are much less human, much more person-ifications, and the story of their birth is an allegory (a symbolic story or picture in which every detail has a meaning that must be interpreted). This fits with Milton's belief that evil has no real existence (see page 13), but do you nevertheless find Sin in particular too human and sympathetic? Her predicament is by any human standards both pitiable and unjustly inflicted. One can quite understand why she disobeys a God *Who hates me* (2:857). But we should read her and Death as a detailed allegory of these words from the first Epistle of James:

> Then when lust hath conceived, it bringeth forth sin: and sin, when it is finished, bringeth forth death.
>
> (I James 1:15)

Satan's *bold conspiracy against Heaven's King* (2:751) can be seen as a kind of lust or desire for power. It leaps out of his head in the form of a woman, as a kind of 'false creation' (see page 168); in effect Satan, not God, invented sin. Satan then falls in love with his own creation (*Thyself in me thy perfect image viewing*, 764), which demonstrates allegorically that sin is a kind of self-love. Their child is Death, because all sin destroys humanity's healthy nature. The theme of self-reflection is continued when Death rapes his mother, and their children, the hell-hounds, continue the rape by kennelling in her womb (658). Allegorically this story suggests that self-love can only lead to inner chaos and decay, and to the false fertility which is the opposite of true creative love.

On a mythic level, however, this Sin is more significant than ordinary human acts of sin. The sin of Adam and Eve *Brought death into the world* (1:3) and, as Satan is responsible for the committing of that sin, he is shown here as the father of Death, and about to release Death and Sin into the world. This is allegorized when they build a road to get to Earth to devour humankind, and for sinners to travel down to Hell for punishment (2:1023–32; see 10:252–61). Satan, Sin and Death form a kind of unity, a demonic trinity, in opposition to the Holy Trinity of Father, Son and Holy Spirit, and Sin even looks forward to sitting on Satan's right, as Christ sits on God's right hand, *Thy daughter and thy darling, without end* (2:870; see Luke 22:69).

'Satan, Sin, and Death: Satan Comes to the Gates of Hell' by William Blake, c. 1806; Sin is half-serpent, and her son Death is semi-transparent

Chaos and Night are less complex. Milton is using the classical idea that matter, in a very confused and violent form, existed before the creation of the world (see the chart on page 11). To give such a disordered world a ruler would be a contradiction in terms, so Milton invents an *anarch* (2:988, from *anarchy*, meaning 'without rule'), who, rather than ruling, *embroils the fray* (908). His age suggests not only that Chaos precedes all the worlds with form (such as Hell and Earth), but also that he is weak and incompetent. His speech is *faltering* (989), and he complains that he was unable to prevent God from raiding his territory to create new worlds.

Logically, Chaos should be a good, or at least a neutral character, since matter all comes ultimately from God. But it suits Milton's plot to make him a supporter of Satan, once the *subtle fiend* (815) has promised to reduce Earth *To her original darkness and your sway* (984). Chaos does not realize that Satan will say anything to get his help in finding Earth, and that if this promise comes true at all, it will only be figuratively.

Milton follows Hesiod, a Greek writer on the gods, in giving Chaos a *consort* (963) or wife, Night. She is equally negative, suggesting the darkness which is the opposite to God and to ordered life. Like Sin, she is female and easily deceived (see the Activity on Hell as a female body on pages 161–2). Chaos and Night are surrounded by other personifications who are clearly influenced by Hesiod and by Vergil's account of the underworld (963–7; see Appendix page 198). But the real ruler in this half-imaginary world is Chance (910), because any other rule would impose order on chaos; note that it is only by chance that Satan crosses the underworld at all (935). The story should be read literally – this is a real journey across a real space – but these personified characters do not have the realism of Satan or even Sin, and we cannot care about them in the same way.

Activity

What does the *fatal key* (2:871) suggest to you?

Discussion

Keys are often symbolic, partly because the insertion of a key in a door suggests the sexual act. This key was given to Sin by God (2:775), with *charge* to keep the devils shut inside Hell (see the illustration on page 161). Once Satan realizes this (815–16), he uses his most persuasive flattery and promises (which are not altogether deceitful) to induce her to disobey God and open the door. This directly anticipates Satan's later realization that the fruit of the Forbidden Tree is the 'key' to the Fall of humankind, and that he must use all his power to persuade Eve (like Sin, a woman) to eat it. Allegorically then, the key, like the fruit, represents the choice between good and evil – the choice which is itself the key to understanding the poem as a whole.

Milton and the Gothic

The Gothic is a literary and aesthetic movement associated at first with the medieval or 'Gothic' revival in art, architecture and literature, initiated by Horace Walpole in 1764 with his pseudo-medieval novel *The Castle of Otranto*. It is therefore quite anachronistic to talk of *Paradise Lost* as a Gothic text, and certain central aspects of Milton's poem (notably his classical form and his religious theme) are alien to the Gothic aesthetic. However, there is no doubt that Milton influenced many texts that can fairly be classed as Gothic: the Creature in Mary Shelley's *Frankenstein* (1818) and Heathcliff in Emily Brontë's *Wuthering Heights* (1847) are only two examples of nineteenth-century anti-heroes who owe a good deal to Milton's Satan.

It can therefore be illuminating to look at *Paradise Lost* through the lens of the Gothic, as it developed in literature of the nineteenth and twentieth centuries.

Features of the Gothic

A list of some of the features of the genre is given below, referring both to passages from later texts that illustrate these features, and to passages from Books 1 and 2 that might have some correspondences with them, so that you can make your own comparisons.

- **An exotic setting**, which according to Kenneth Clark 'if not remote in space, is remote in time' (*The Gothic Revival*, 1928). Castles, nunneries, and distant islands are the location for strange adventures; it is the landscape of dreams. Thus *Frankenstein* begins in the Arctic with a description of a terrifying fairy-tale ogre roaming across the ice. Milton begins his poem in Hell, and includes a frightening journey to a land of ice (2:587–628) and another across Chaos (2:890–950). It could be said that such grand landscapes elevate as well as terrify us; as Edmund Burke put it in 1757, 'whatever is in any sort terrible... is a source of the *sublime*, that is, it is productive of the strongest emotion' (*On the Sublime*, quoted in *The Gothic Novel: A Casebook*, page 33; see Further Reading page 195).

• **An adventure at once fantastic and horrific**, so that the author's imagination seems to be released simply to frighten readers. The presence of the uncanny in such fictions is said by psychologists to reveal 'what should have remained hidden and secret' (*The Gothic Novel: A Casebook*, page 77). Consciously medieval texts, such as S.T. Coleridge's *Christabel* (1816), use the supernatural in their plots, making them like fairy tales; more recent authors use pseudo-science to awaken the dead or distort the living into the stuff of nightmare. Are Milton's Sin and Death, who are both disgusting and unnatural, frightening in the same way?

• **Villains who are divided and alienated.** Heathcliff in *Wuthering Heights* is directly compared to Satan when Cathy says: 'Your cruelty arises from your greater misery... [you are] lonely, like the devil, and envious like him' (Chapter 29); the Creature in *Frankenstein* begs his creator for a wife (Volume II Chapter 9) and, in his despair, paraphrases Milton's Satan: 'Evil thenceforth became my good' (Volume III Chapter 7). Such characters, though pitiable, are generally wholly evil in their effects on the plot. The heroes themselves, such as Dr Jekyll in Robert Louis Stevenson's *Dr Jekyll and Mr Hyde* (1886), or Victor Frankenstein in Mary Shelley's novel, are often cursed with a Faustian ambition which prompts them to 'play God' and so to release a darker self and to degenerate morally; this is discussed in David Punter's influential *The Literature of Terror* Volume 2; see Further Reading, page 195). Does Satan, *Vaunting aloud, but racked with deep despair, who trusted to have equalled the most High* (1:126, 40), combine both these aspects, and does he strike the reader as wholly evil in his effects?

- **Good characters who are wholly good**, but weak, powerless, innocent, and so at the mercy of the evil characters. This reinforces the fairy-tale quality already present through the use of the supernatural. Although generally good wins in the end, we can feel the presence of a distorted sexual violence. Milton's Sin is a passive woman, but can she be said to evoke our sympathy like Lucy in Bram Stoker's *Dracula*? Do you feel that good will triumph in the end?

However you choose to use Milton's reflections in Gothic literature, do not forget that he preceded this genre by at least a century, and that the differences between his work and these later texts are greater than the similarities.

Critical views

Milton has had an enormous influence on English writers. The eighteenth-century poets imitated his style and poetic diction – to the extent, according to T.S. Eliot, that they could no longer reflect common experience (he called this the 'dissociation of sensibility'). The Romantics tried to return to the 'language of men', by which they meant ordinary people (William Wordsworth's *Preface to the Lyrical Ballads*, 1800), but fell under the spell of Milton's characters and ideas. The early Romantic poet William Blake was inspired by *Paradise Lost* to write his *Songs of Innocence and Experience* (1794), but he took issue with Milton's religious morality, which is of course derived from the Old Testament, and saw Satan as the true hero of the poem, famously saying that:

> The reason Milton wrote in fetters when he wrote of Angels & God, and at liberty when of Devils & Hell, is because he was a true poet, and of the Devil's party without knowing it.
> *(Marriage of Heaven and Hell,* 1790)

The poet Percy Shelley also found Satan to be 'as a moral being… far superior to God' (*Defence of Poetry*, 1821) and his wife Mary transformed him into the Creature in *Frankenstein* (see page 182).

These correspondences are explored in Lucy Newlyn's *Paradise Lost and the Romantic Reader* (1993).

Twentieth-century responses have continued this attack on the religious and mythic level of the poem. In what became known as the 'Milton controversy', the writer and critic C.S. Lewis (author of a science-fiction version of the poem, *Perelandra*), represented the Christian position in *A Preface to Paradise Lost* (1961, based on lectures given in 1941, see the next page). William Empson represented the humanist atheist view in *Milton's God* (1961), supported by critics such as T.S. Eliot, who even asserts:

> So far as I perceive anything, it is a glimpse of a theology that I find in large part repellent, expressed through a mythology which would have been better left in the Book of Genesis, upon which Milton has not improved.
>
> (Essay of 1936, reprinted in *On Poetry and Poets*, 1957, 144)

In a close analysis of Books 1 and 2, Empson argues that God has tricked Satan into continuing to resist him, by allowing the war in Heaven to continue for three days:

> The belief that he has proved God not to be omnipotent is so rooted in his mind that... we find it permeating almost every clause of his defence.
>
> (*Milton's God*, page 44)

Some of the chief writings of the Milton controversy and its aftermath can be found in *Paradise Lost: A Casebook* edited by J.E. Dyson and J. Lovelock (1973), and in J.M. Evans's *John Milton: Twentieth-century Perspectives* (2003). But many of the objections made to Milton's religious ideas have been allayed by more recent research. Both Eliot and Empson were countered by Dennis Danielson in *Milton's Good God* (1982), a careful consideration of Milton's religious ideas in the light of seventeenth-century controversies. J.M. Evans and John Broadbent have examined his relation to mythology, and Stephen Fallon has further contextualized his philosophy, pointing out for example that it was because Milton did not believe in the actual existence of evil as a principle opposed to God (see discussion on page 13) that Sin and Death have a 'lesser reality as allegorical characters' (*Milton Among the Philosophers*, page 171). See Further Reading for full references to these studies.

F.R. Leavis followed Eliot in extending the attack into Milton's style, which he said was responsible for 'the extreme and consistent remoteness of Milton's medium from any English that was ever spoken' (essay entitled 'Milton's Verse', in *Scrutiny*, 1933). His views were endorsed by others, but recent critics have been much more enthusiastic about Milton's idiosyncratic but exciting brand of English poetry, and there are now many studies that give appreciative analyses of Books 1 and 2. Christopher Ricks, in the useful short study entitled *Milton's Grand Style* (1963) – a phrase first used satirically by Leavis – discusses his rhythms, syntax, metaphors, word-play and use of puns, and coins the phrase 'liquid syntax' to describe Milton's deliberately ambiguous grammar (page 79). Alternative approaches are offered by Catherine Belsey, in *John Milton: Language, Gender, Power*, which approaches the poem through modern critical theory, or in the anthology of critical readings edited by Annabel Patterson (*Milton*, 1992). In *Paradise Lost and the Rhetoric of Literary Forms*, Barbara Lewalski discusses the use of rhetoric in the poem.

The divided views on Satan that were epitomized by the Blake quotation at the beginning of this section persist. During the Milton controversy, C.S. Lewis, writing from a moral and religious standpoint, saw Satan as a self-absorbed, self-contradicting and ultimately absurd character:

> What we see in Satan is the terrible co-existence of a subtle and incessant intellectual activity and an incapacity to understand anything... His monomaniac concern with himself and his supposed rights and wrongs is a necessity of the Satanic predicament... He is interesting to read about, but Milton makes plain the blank uninterestingness of *being* Satan.
>
> (*A Preface to Paradise Lost*, 99, 102)

In *Paradise Lost and its Critics* (1947), A.J.A. Waldock countered Lewis, arguing that Milton's comments on Satan are at variance with the actual effect of the character on our sympathies and even our capacity for admiration:

> He will put some glorious thing in Satan's mouth, and then, anxious about the effect of it, will pull us gently by the sleeve, saying... 'Do not be carried away by this fellow; he *sounds* splendid, but take my word for it...'
>
> *(Paradise Lost and its Critics,* page 78)

Helen Gardner also countered Lewis, arguing in 'Milton's Satan and the Theme of Damnation in Elizabethan Tragedy' (1948, reprinted in *Milton: Modern Essays in Criticism*, ed. A.E. Barker) that Satan is essentially a tragic hero, of the same kind as Shakespeare's Macbeth or Marlowe's Doctor Faustus (see Appendix page 200). The egotism that Lewis deplores is characteristic of such heroes, and we are 'held enthralled by the voice of Hamlet' as we are by the voice of Satan because of and not in spite of his ability to express his own predicament. Milton, like Shakespeare, does not gloss over the evil in his tragic heroes, and it is this that makes them truly doomed.

Another alternative to Lewis's Christian response to Satan is provided by critics like David Loewenstein or Charles Martindale, who set the poem in its classical context. So, in his useful little guide to the poem, Loewenstein gives a detailed account of Satan in Books 1 and 2 as a classical hero:

> Speaking with the pride, rage and vengefulness of an Achilles, he reveals his pagan sensibility – his aggression and values resembling those of the combative, daring warrior of classical epic.
>
> *(Milton's Paradise Lost,* page 57)

However, Loewenstein also indicates Milton's departures from this tradition, in giving Satan the inward torment which motivates his tyranny and deceit of others. Martindale, in *John Milton and the Transformation of Ancient Epic*, also insists that Milton does not plagiarize, but rather transforms his classical sources; in contrast F.C. Blessington (see Further Reading) finds parallels between Satan's situation and that of the source characters. To Martindale, for example, Satan's first words to Beëlzebub must have recalled to many of Milton's readers Aeneas's description of the ghost of Hector ('Alas how he looked – how changed from the Hector clad in the spoils of Achilles...'), but we are not meant to see either Satan or Beëlzebub as types of virtue like Hector and Aeneas. Another striking parallel to Satan's situation can be found in Greek drama, between Satan on his lake of fire and Prometheus, the heroic opponent of Zeus, pinned to a rock for daring to steal fire for humankind, in Aeschylus's play *Prometheus Bound* (see the discussion on page 170).

You should ask yourself whether you see Satan as either a classical or a Shakespearean hero, or as essentially unheroic (as Lewis argued). Do the heroism and suffering that are so clearly evident in Satan's speeches in Book 1 make up for the unscrupulousness of the plots against humankind, or the deceit of all those whom he encounters on his journey to Earth, in Book 2? As with so many of the critical views discussed here, there is a choice between those who focus on Milton's dramatically sympathetic portrayal of characters, and those who see the moral and intellectual impetus of the poem condemning those same characters.

Finally, many critics contextualize *Paradise Lost* in seventeenth-century history, and look at the part Milton played in it. One of the most readable authors on this is Christopher Hill, who suggests in *Milton and the English Revolution* that Satan is modelled not so much on Oliver Cromwell the rebel, as on Charles I the tyrant king. He argues that, as Books 1–6 were probably written before the restoration of Charles II in 1660, 'Satan's attempt *Against the omnipotent to rise in arms* (6:136) seemed as absurd as a Royalist attempt to reverse the verdict of history' (pages 365–6).

The more usual position is taken by Robert Fallon in *Divided Empire*; his interesting chapter on the 'Great Consult' pairs Satan with Oliver Cromwell. Satan's position as 'first among equals', unable to dictate policy but requiring the free assent of his fellow angels, is like Cromwell's position in September 1651, 'as he returned from his victories over Ireland, Scotland and the royalist forces of Charles II to resume his seat on the Commonwealth Council' (page 64). Does Satan's ability to manipulate the council to vote for his own plan rather than Belial's suggest a criticism of Cromwell's methods, or is Milton simply remembering the realities of the Commonwealth experiment?

Other authors, such as Peter Levi in *Eden Renewed: The Public and Private Life of John Milton* and A.N. Wilson in *A Life of John Milton*, focus their study of historical context on Milton's own life. Anna Beer in *Milton: Poet, Pamphleteer and Patriot* sets the poetry within the context of Milton's own political writing. However, you may prefer simply to look at contemporary documents and judge for yourself whether they are relevant to Books 1 and 2. The Putney Debates of 1647, for example, provide a fascinating context for the debate in Hell, although Milton was much more traditionalist in his views than some of the radicals who argued for a genuine democracy without distinction of property and class. Excerpts from the Putney Debates can be read in David Wootton's anthology of contemporary documents called *Divine Right and Democracy*. Another useful collection can be found in *John Milton's Paradise Lost: A Sourcebook* edited by Margaret Kean, which gives excerpts from contemporary documents and from recent critics, as well as from the poem itself, all well introduced. For all these books, see Further Reading.

Essay Questions

1 What features of Satan's appearance and character contribute to our understanding of him as *archangel ruined* (1:593) and the hero rather than the villain of Books 1 and 2?

2 *Vaunting aloud, but racked with deep despair* (1:126). How does Milton convey these two sides to Satan's character?

3 Milton often describes Satan as the *subtle fiend* (2:815). Look at his manipulation both of the truth and of other people in his speeches.

4 Using some historical context in your answer, say whether you think that Books 1 and 2 indicate that Milton was, as Blake claims, 'of the Devil's party without knowing it'.

5 Joseph Addison regarded Milton's biblical and classical references as 'an unnecessary ostentation of learning'. How far do you agree? Make close reference to Books 1 and 2 in your response.

6 How do the speeches made by Moloch, Belial and Mammon in Book 2 relate to the descriptions that Milton gives of their characters in Book 1?

7 Compare 1:44–75 or 2:587–628 with Mephistopheles' speeches from *Dr Faustus* quoted in the Appendix (page 200). How does each suggest that Hell is both outside and within the human mind?

8 Compare 1:622–62 (Satan's speech to his fallen army) with Hitler's election speech of 1932 (Appendix page 201). What do they share, and how are they different?

9 'A study in corrupted ambition.' How far is this true of the depiction of Satan in Books 1 and 2?

10 Is it illuminating to see Milton as the grandfather of nineteenth-century Gothic literature? Make close reference to Books 1 and 2 in your response.

Class Activities

Frieze from Book 1

Make a frieze of the chief fallen angels, now devils, using the parade of 1:376–521. You can draw them yourselves, or use magazine pictures to make collages (Ashtaroth, for example, is both male and female). Each student should be responsible for one god, and write a brief description in modern terms of his or her particular viciousness.

Debate from Book 2

Imagine that you are fallen angels; hold your own debate on the question 'Should we continue the war against God?' As far as possible, use the arguments expressed in 2:43–283. The following could be used as starting points by different students, who should also incorporate additional quotations and modern equivalents.

1 The place. Should we *Accept this dark opprobrious den of shame* (58)?

2 Our death. Are we hoping for extinction *happier far/Than miserable to have eternal being* (97–8)? Or would it be terrible to be *swallowed up and lost/In the wide womb of uncreated night* (149–50)?

3 Our suffering. Are we in fact suffering or in despair *when the scourge/ Inexorably, and the torturing hour/Call us to penance* (90–2), or are we not too unhappy *Thus sitting, thus consulting, thus in arms* (164)?

4 Our freedom. Are we *In strictest bondage… Under th'inevitable curb* (321–2), or are we in effect freer than in the *splendid vassalage* of Heaven (252)?

5 Our creativity. Should we be trying to frustrate God's plans to *interrupt his joy* (371), or should we try to build something positive in Hell, *Nor want we skill or art* (272)?

6 Our honour. Should we heroically continue the fight *Turning our tortures into horrid arms/Against the Torturer* (63–4) or is this pointless since *fate inevitable/ Subdues us* (197–8)?

Chronology

Further Reading

Historical, contextual and biographical studies

Anna Beer, *Milton: Poet, Pamphleteer and Patriot* (Bloomsbury, 2008)

F.C. Blessington, *Paradise Lost and the Classical Epic* (Routledge, 1979)

Gordon Campbell, *John Milton* (*Very Interesting People* Series, Oxford University Press, 2007)

J.M. Evans, *Paradise Lost and the Genesis Tradition* (Oxford University Press, 1968)

Robert T. Fallon, *Divided Empire: Milton's Political Imagery* (Pennsylvania State University Press, 1995)

Stephen M. Fallon, *Milton Among the Philosophers* (Cornell University Press, 1991)

Christopher Hill, *Milton and the English Revolution* (Faber and Faber, 1977)

Margaret Kean (ed.), *John Milton's Paradise Lost: A Sourcebook* (Routledge, 2005)

Peter Levi, *Eden Renewed: The Public and Private Life of John Milton* (Macmillan, 1996)

Charles Martindale, *John Milton and the Transformation of Ancient Epic* (Rowman & Littlefield, 1986)

Lois Potter, *A Preface to Milton* (Longman, 1971, revised 1986)

A.N. Wilson, *A Life of John Milton* (Oxford University Press, 1983)

David Wootton (ed.), *Divine Right and Democracy: An Anthology of Political Writing in Stuart England* (Penguin, 1986)

Introductions and collections of critical essays

A.E. Barker (ed.), *Milton: Modern Essays in Criticism* (Oxford University Press, 1965)

F.C. Blessington (ed.), *Paradise Lost: A Student's Companion to the Poem* (Twayne, 1988)

Dennis Danielson (ed.), *The Cambridge Companion to Milton* (Cambridge University Press, 1989)

Angelica Duran (ed.), *A Concise Companion to Milton* (Blackwell, 2007)

J.E. Dyson and J. Lovelock (eds.), *Milton's Paradise Lost: A Casebook* (Macmillan, 1973)

J.M. Evans (ed.), *John Milton: Twentieth-century Perspectives* (Routledge, 2003)

Louis L. Martz (ed.), *Milton: A Collection of Critical Essays* (Prentice-Hall, 1966)

Annabel Patterson (ed.), *Milton* (Longman's Critical Readers, 1992)

Geoff Ridden, *Paradise Lost Books I and II* (York Notes Advanced, 2000)

Joseph Wittreich, *Why Milton Matters: A New Preface to his Writings* (Palgrave Macmillan, 2006)

William Zunder, *Paradise Lost: John Milton* (New Casebooks, Palgrave Macmillan, 1999)

Longer critical studies

John Broadbent, *Paradise Lost: An Introduction* (Cambridge University Press, 1972)

Catherine Belsey, *John Milton: Language, Gender, Power* (Blackwell, 1988)

Dennis Danielson, *Milton's Good God* (Cambridge University Press, 1982)

William Empson, *Milton's God* (Chatto and Windus, 1961)

B.K. Lewalski, *Paradise Lost and the Rhetoric of Literary Forms* (Princeton University Press, 1985)

C.S. Lewis, *A Preface to Paradise Lost* (Oxford University Press, 1961)

David Loewenstein, *Milton's Paradise Lost: Landmarks of World Literature* (Cambridge University Press, 2003)

Christopher Ricks, *Milton's Grand Style* (Clarendon Press, 1963)

A.J.A. Waldock, *Paradise Lost and its Critics* (Cambridge University Press, 1947)

Peter Weston, *John Milton: Paradise Lost* (Penguin Critical Studies, 1987)

The Gothic

Lucy Newlyn, *Paradise Lost and the Romantic Reader* (Oxford University Press, 1993)

David Punter, *The Literature of Terror* (Longman, 1980)

Victor Sage (ed.), *The Gothic Novel: A Casebook* (Macmillan, 1990)

Other editions of Books 1 and 2

John Broadbent (ed.), *Paradise Lost Books I–II* (Cambridge University Press, 1972)

Alastair Fowler (ed.), *Milton: Paradise Lost* (Longman, 1968)

F.T. Prince (ed.), *Paradise Lost Books I and II* (Oxford University Press, 1962)

Recording

John Milton: Paradise Lost read by Anton Lesser (Naxos AudioBooks, 1994, reissued 2006): can be purchased as partial (including Book 1 and most of Book 2) or complete poem.

Appendix 1

Bible passages believed to refer to Satan

These quotations are taken from the Authorized Version of 1611; words from this translation often appear in Milton's poem, and it would have been well-known to his audience. This version has also been used in the Notes.

These parts of the Bible were brought together to make the story of the Fall of Satan and the Fall of Adam and Eve (see page 12). Do you think Milton's characterization is consistent with these sources?

> Revelation 12:7–9: And there was war in heaven: Michael and his angels fought against the dragon; and the dragon fought and his angels... And the great dragon was cast out, that old serpent, called the Devil, and Satan, which deceiveth the whole world: he was cast out into the earth, and his angels were cast out with him.

> Isaiah 14:12–15: How art thou fallen from heaven, O Lucifer, son of the morning!... For thou hast said in thine heart, I will ascend into heaven, I will exalt my throne above the stars of God... I will ascend above the heights of the clouds; I will be like the most High. Yet thou shalt be brought down to hell, to the sides of the pit.

> Genesis 3:1–6: Now the serpent was more subtil than any beast of the field which the Lord God had made. And he said unto the woman, Yea, hath God said, Ye shall not eat of every tree of the garden? And the woman said unto the serpent, We may eat of the fruit of the trees of the garden: but of the fruit of the tree which is in the midst of the garden, God hath said, Ye shall not eat of it, neither shall ye touch it, lest ye die. And the serpent said unto the woman, Ye shall not surely die: for God doth know that in the day ye eat thereof, then your eyes shall be opened, and ye shall be as gods, knowing good and evil. And when the

woman saw that the tree was good for food, and that it was pleasant to the eyes, and a tree to be desired to make one wise, she took of the fruit thereof, and did eat, and gave also unto her husband with her; and he did eat.

Genesis 3:23: ... therefore the Lord God sent him forth from the garden of Eden, to till the ground from whence he was taken.

Appendix 2

Aeschylus, *Prometheus Bound* 89–114: The suffering god

This play, believed to have been first performed in the 450s BC in Athens, would have been read by Milton in Greek. He might have found in its portrayal of a deposed Titan, punished by Zeus for giving fire to humankind, a model for Satan's defiance in the face of an apparently unending punishment by God (see the discussion in Interpretations page 170). It is more usual, however, to see Prometheus as a prototype for the suffering Christ.

(Prometheus is left alone on the rock)
Prometheus: Bright light, swift-winged winds, springs of the rivers, numberless
laughter of the sea's waves, earth, mother of all, and the all-seeing
circle of the sun: I call upon you to see what I, a God, suffer
at the hands of Gods –
see what kind of torture
worn down I shall wrestle ten thousand
years of time –
such is the despiteful bond that the Prince
has devised against me, the new Prince
of the Blessed Ones. Oh woe is me!
I groan for the present sorrow,
I groan for the sorrow to come, I groan

questioning when there shall come a time
when He shall ordain a limit to my sufferings.
What am I saying? I have known all before,
all that shall be, and clearly known; to me,
nothing that hurts shall come with a new face.
So must I bear, as lightly as I can,
the destiny that fate has given me;
for I know well against necessity,
against its strength, no one can fight and win.

I cannot speak about my fortune, cannot
hold my tongue either. It was mortal man
to whom I gave great privileges and
for that was yoked in this unyielding harness.
I hunted out the secret spring of fire,
that filled the narthex stem, which when revealed
became the teacher of each craft to men,
a great resource. This is the sin committed
for which I stand accountant, and I pay
nailed in my chains under the open sky.

(Translated by David Grene, in *Aeschylus II, The Complete Greek Tragedies* series, ed. D. Grene and R. Lattimore, Chicago University Press, 1991)

Appendix 3

Vergil, *Aeneid* Book 6, 271–314: Descent into the underworld

Vergil's epic poem, the *Aeneid*, written in Rome in the first century BC, was an important influence on *Paradise Lost* (see Interpretations page 150). The following passage, taken from Aeneas's descent into the underworld, has several ideas which Milton uses in Books 1 and 2 (see the discussion on page 152).

Before the entrance, in the jaws of Orcus,
Grief and avenging Cares have made their beds,
And pale Diseases and sad Age are there,
And Dread, and Hunger that sways men to crime,
5   And sordid Want – in shapes to affright the eyes –
And Death and Toil and Death's own brother, Sleep,
And the mind's evil joys; on the door sill
Death-bringing War, and iron cubicles
Of the Eumenidës, and raving Discord,
10 Viperish hair bound up in gory bands.
In the courtyard a shadowy giant elm
Spreads ancient boughs, her ancient arms where dreams,
False dreams, the old tale goes, beneath each leaf
Cling and are numberless. There, too,
15 About the doorway forms of monsters crowd –
Centaurs, twiformed Scyllas, hundred-armed
Briareus, and the Lernaean hydra
Hissing horribly, and the Chimaera
Breathing dangerous flames, and Gorgons, Harpies,
20 Huge Geryon, triple-bodied ghost.
Here, swept by sudden fear, drawing his sword,
Aeneas stood on guard with naked edge
Against them as they came. If his companion,
Knowing the truth, had not admonished him
25 How faint these lives were – empty images
Hovering bodiless – he had attacked
And cut his way through phantoms, empty air.

The path goes on from that place to the waves
Of Tartarus's Acheron...

30 Here a whole crowd came streaming to the banks,
Mothers and men, the forms with all life spent
Of heroes great in valor, boys and girls
Unmarried, and young sons laid on the pyre
Before their parents' eyes – as many souls
35 As leaves that yield their hold on boughs and fall

> Through forests in the early frost of autumn,
> Or as migrating birds from the open sea
> That darken heaven when the cold season comes
> And drives them overseas to sunlit lands.
> 40 There all stood begging to be first across
> And reached out longing hands to the far shore.

(Translated by Robert Fitzgerald in *The Aeneid*, Random House, 1983)

Appendix 4

Marlowe, *Dr Faustus*: The Hell within

The English representation of the devil which probably had most influence on Milton was that of Mephistopheles from Christopher Marlowe's play *Dr Faustus* (1592). Like Satan, Mephistopheles inhabits a mental as well as a physical Hell and he is unhappy because he is deprived of God. In the following extracts Faustus, a magician, has just called Mephistopheles from Hell and is questioning him. See Interpretations pages 167 and 175 and Essay Questions.

Faustus: Tell me what is that Lucifer thy lord?
Mephistopheles: Arch-regent and commander of all spirits.
Faustus: Was not that Lucifer an angel once?
Mephistopheles: Yes, Faustus, and most dearly loved of God.
Faustus: How comes it then that he is prince of devils?
Mephistopheles: O, by aspiring pride and insolence,
For which God threw him from the face of heaven.
Faustus: And what are you that live with Lucifer?
Mephistopheles: Unhappy spirits that fell with Lucifer,
Conspired against our God with Lucifer,
And are forever damned with Lucifer.
Faustus: Where are you damned?
Mephistopheles: In hell.
Faustus: How comes it then that thou are out of hell?
Mephistopheles: Why, this is hell, nor am I out of it.

Think'st thou that I, who saw the face of God
And tasted the eternal joys of heaven,
Am not tormented with ten thousand hells
In being deprived of everlasting bliss?
O Faustus, leave these frivolous demands
Which strike a terror to my fainting soul!

(I.3.64–84)

Mephistopheles: Now, Faustus, ask what thou wilt.
Faustus: First will I question with thee about hell.
Tell me, where is the place that men call hell?
Mephistopheles: Under the heavens.
Faustus: Ay, but whereabout?
Mephistopheles: Within the bowels of these elements,
Where we are tortured and remain for ever.
Hell hath no limits, nor is circumscribed
In one self place, for where we are is hell,
And where hell is must we ever be.
And, to conclude, when all the world dissolves,
And every creature shall be purified,
All places shall be hell that is not heaven.
Faustus: Come, I think hell's a fable.
Mephistopheles: Ay, think so still, till experience change thy mind.

(II.1.119–32)

Appendix 5

Adolf Hitler: Speech to the Industry Club in Dusseldorf, 1932

Hitler gave the speech from which this extract is taken during his first election campaign of 1932, when he promised a recovery from present economic hardship, caused by defeat in the First World War, to those who would support the Nazi party. See Essay Questions page 190.

Today we stand at the turning-point of Germany's destiny. If the present development continues, Germany will one day of necessity land in Bolshevist chaos, but if this development is broken, then our people must be taken into a school of iron discipline and gradually freed...

Even if another batch of twenty emergency decrees is rained down on our people, these will not stay the great line which leads to destruction, but if one day the road be discovered which leads upwards, then first of all the German people must be bent straight again. That is a process which none can escape! It is no good to say that the proletarians are alone responsible. No, believe me, our whole German people of all ranks has a full measure of responsibility for our collapse – a measure pressed down and running over – some because they willed it and have consciously sought to bring it about, the others because they looked on and were too weak to stop our downfall. In history the failure to act is weighed as strictly as is the purpose or the deed. Today no one can escape the obligation to complete the regeneration of the German body-politic: every one must show his personal sympathy, must take his place in the common effort.

(From *The Penguin Book of Twentieth-Century Speeches*, ed. Brian MacArthur, Viking, 1992, pages 116–17)